GHOSTS

GHOSTS

An Investigation into a True Canadian Haunting

Richard Palmisano

DUNDURN PRESS
TORONTO

Editor: Shannon Whibbs
Designer: Jennifer Scott
Printer: Webcom

Library and Archives Canada Cataloguing in Publication

Palmisano, Richard
    Ghosts : an investigation into a true Canadian haunting / by Richard Palmisano.

ISBN 978-1-55488-435-3

1. Ghosts--Ontario. 2. Haunted houses--Ontario--Mississauga. I. Title.

BF1472.C3P328 2009   133.1'09713535   C2009-902465-9

1 2 3 4 5   13 12 11 10 09

  Conseil des Arts   Canada Council   Canadä   ONTARIO ARTS COUNCIL
du Canada   for the Arts   CONSEIL DES ARTS DE L'ONTARIO

We acknowledge the support of the **Canada Council for the Arts** and the **Ontario Arts Council** for our publishing program. We also acknowledge the financial support of the **Government of Canada** through the **Book Publishing Industry Development Program** and **The Association for the Export of Canadian Books,** and the **Government of Ontario** through the **Ontario Book Publishers Tax Credit program,** and the **Ontario Media Development Corporation**.

Care has been taken to trace the ownership of copyright material used in this book. The author and the publisher welcome any information enabling them to rectify any references or credits in subsequent editions.

J. Kirk Howard, President

Printed and bound in Canada.
www.dundurn.com

All visuals are courtesy of Richard Palmisano unless credited otherwise.

Dundurn Press	Gazelle Book Services Limited	Dundurn Press
3 Church Street, Suite 500	White Cross Mills	2250 Military Road
Toronto, Ontario, Canada	High Town, Lancaster, England	Tonawanda, NY
M5E 1M2	LA1 4XS	U.S.A. 14150

Mixed Sources
Product group from well-managed forests, and other controlled sources
www.fsc.org Cert no. SW-COC-002358
FSC © 1996 Forest Stewardship Council

CONTENTS

To see what is beyond the eye.
To hear without your ears.
Push past all senses and defy,
All of your greatest fears.

For once you have then you will see,
More clearly than before.
Now in your grasp you have the key,
To open a new door.

— AMANDA JOBE

PREFACE

Since the beginning of recorded history, humankind has been aware of ghosts, or at least aware of the stories about ghosts brought forth by witnesses to these strange and sometimes frightening phenomena. Many have tried to explain what ghosts are, and there are numerous theories — all unproven. Nevertheless, these strange stories have forged our faith and our fears, many becoming the tales we tell each other on moonlit nights around a campfire. Hollywood has (as it normally does on any subject that affects the human condition) taken a great deal of the good work done on life-after-death research and twisted it into a horror fest, so that when most people think of ghosts they automatically envision terrifying images; things that make up our nightmares. These images are so far removed from the truth that we have little choice but to fear them. I am not saying that there are not malevolent forces out there, because there are. However, most spirits are quite benevolent souls who have little interest in us. One must remember that these souls are the reflection of the person they once were. The greatest misconception is that these spirits roam aimlessly, looking for some poor unsuspecting person to torment and haunt — not true. As they have a very active life beyond their physical death, they hardly have time to bother with the living. They seem to be very social in their new existence.

The Searcher Group is a Canadian-owned company whose membership has been assembled to focus on making advancements in parapsychology — specifically research into the existence of life after death. What is our interest in ghosts and life after death? When I ask people, they tell me it's interesting, exciting, and scary. I accept those general answers, however superficial, as I feel the deeper interest is that we all think, at one time or another, about our mortality and wonder if there is more to life and, yes, more beyond our physical death. Many people seek out the answers in books and documentaries on a personal quest of discovery, some don't discuss the subject, and others will quietly talk with a friend or relative they have come to realize have the same questions. In a multicultural society where discussions of a religious nature are practically taboo, it is difficult to pursue the answers one is searching for in open forums. This is in part why The Searcher Group was formed, as a medium to provide information and assistance to people looking for help.

The main mission of The Searcher Group is twofold: the first is to preserve our history and the history of those who have gone on before us, and the second is to assist people who are faced with paranormal phenomena and find it difficult to cope with these ongoing situations. The Searcher Group assists by providing education, intervention, or conflict resolution. When dealing with hauntings and the spirit world there are a great number of unknown factors, and this is inherently true when dealing with human personalities and their personal intentions toward others.

For us to provide the best possible help we rely heavily upon the generosity of various levels of government and property owners who allow us to study and work in historical properties and abandoned buildings to gather data, test theories, and conduct experiments. Without their trust and permission we would not be able to provide the services that we offer. The Searcher Group never charges for their services and all costs are paid directly by the team members.

Anyone wishing to contact the Searcher Group or the author may do so by e-mail (*overshadows@sympatico.ca*). Please do not send attachments, as they will automatically be deleted.

I have, in the past, received e-mails asking me why it takes so long for me to write my books. Unlike fiction, we are dealing with historical events and events not well recorded, as well as information hidden in obscure places. These obstacles, coupled with the need to sort out the events of a haunting, create a remarkable and exhaustive project. Once the job is in hand I feel a deep responsibility to tell the story as accurately as possible. All too often I have seen writers compromise the truth in order to rush their book to press. Even in the case of this particular story, I know of an author who, in his rush to produce a book, failed to fully investigate the history of this grand house and reported, for the most part, a great deal of wrong information, which means researchers in the future will automatically have a handicap if the book is used as research material. This only weakens us as we try to raise parapsychology up to the level of respectability it deserves. Every care has been taken to report the events as they occurred or were witnessed. All the events are true, some will find them terrifying, and most will find that there is hope as the journey of life seems to continue on after our physical death. It will be purely up to the reader to decide what that continuation is.

ACKNOWLEDGEMENTS

First and foremost I would like to thank my wife Michelle for her continued support of all the crazy things I do and for her help on this and all of my projects. You could have married someone normal — I could be home right now watching football!

To all the staff at Dundurn, thank you for all of your hard work. Mr. Kirk Howard and Mr. Tony Hawke, thank you for believing in my work.

A big thank-you to all the great people working for the City of Mississauga, especially to Mr. Hillis, and Joe Cairney for having the trust in us to do this work.

Thank you, Chris Harding, for all your help and support with this project.

Thank you to Lloyd Herridge for all your assistance.

Thank you Cathy Jobe for all your time and hard work.

To the team who makes going out on these adventures a joy: Amanda Jobe, Sheryl Popp, John Mullan, John Perrone, Michele Stableford, Lester Hickman, Steve Barwick, Jennifer Brooks, and Ben Rose, I appreciate all of your opinions and hard work. To the participants who worked with us during this project and survived the experiment: Peter Roe, Mark Robinson, Lynn Pinette, John Burnell, and Anthony Popp, thank you.

Thanks to the Hauntings Research Group for their participation, input, and observations: Dee Freedman, Krystal Leigh, and Anita Parron.

Thanks to Scott McClelland for his input and skeptical views.

Thank you to the production team for their assistance and their views: Darrin LePointe, Jason Perez, Justin McIntosh, Grant MacPhee, Robert Mara, Roy Contreras, and Marilyn Barbara.

It is through Paul Palmisano's dedication that a great deal of our EVPs and visual anomalies are discovered. He spends countless hours reviewing our surveillance footage, sometimes frame by frame. He takes on this responsibility to locate and identify recorded artifacts of interest for the rest of the team. Imagine, if you will, a typical one-night investigation that remains in progress for eight hours, with an average of four cameras recording, producing thirty-two hours of audio and videotape to be reviewed and analyzed. Keep in mind that the majority of that material will contain nothing of interest, mostly empty halls and blank walls: imagine having to be the one to take on such a task! The reward for him is when something is captured and he is the first person to hear or see it. The service that he provides is an extremely valuable one for the Searcher Group and I thank him for it.

EXPLANATION

To add continuity to the story I have, in certain instances, included information recorded by surveillance at each of the respective properties as it happens; however, the reader must understand that the information recorded would not be revealed to the investigative team until days later, when the tapes were reviewed and analyzed.

Throughout this book there will be references to EVP. EVP stands for *electronic voice phenomena* — voices and or sounds captured on recording tape that are believed to be those of the dead. EVPs can be extremely persuasive when specific answers are given to direct questions, or when names are given that are later found, through investigation, to have had a relationship with the property in question.

I have included many of the recorded EVP excerpts from our audio surveillance equipment throughout this book so that you may have a better understanding of what the investigative team was encountering during their work on the property. The EVPs also give some clues as to what was taking place within the structures between the spirits and allow some insight into the relationships of those spirits that still remain there.

In most instances EVPs are not heard at the time and the investigative team is only aware of this recorded information after review of the tape or digital recording. On rare occasions single words or parts of a message can be heard audibly by ear at the time of the recording by those present.

Most recordings are made by way of specific surveillance guidelines, whereas audio and video systems are set to record in vacant rooms, and normally the entire house is vacated when these systems are operating to ensure they are not influenced by or interacted with by any of the team members.

Several things made this investigation extraordinary. Looking back over the last three years and the number of recordings made from Fusion and the farm is staggering; of the 640 hours of tape used, we captured an astounding 391 EVPs, and almost a third of those were names and events that correlated directly to real people from the history of these properties. The majority of these EVPs were in real time, acting and reacting to us and our actions as we investigated the interior of both homes, demonstrating that they could perceive us and attempting to interact with us and our equipment at that moment. Most of the EVPs showed a social interaction between the spirits themselves. While the majority were in a positive manner, there were, however, some negative exchanges recorded as well. They demonstrated that there is communication between the spirits on a constant basis: doing chores, taking orders, playing, flirting, and even bouts of anger as if life never stopped for them. It was strange, as if they were lingering between two worlds. The transition between life and the after life for them didn't skip a beat, our interruptions into their everyday routines was unwelcome, possibly a reminder that not all was well and may have brought up the memory that they were no longer physical.

Mediums or clairvoyants are used as a tool to pull information from a haunted location and attempt to communicate with spirits. As an investigator, what they report only holds credence when verified by a second source. A second source could be a historical report, names and or dates that were directly associated with the site, and, or direct recordings of electronic voice phenomena of a spirit stating the same or very similar information as the medium has reported.

Remote viewing is a paranormal ability of a person to use their senses of sight and sound to gain information from a distant location, whereas the viewer is not in physical attendance.

FLOOR PLANS

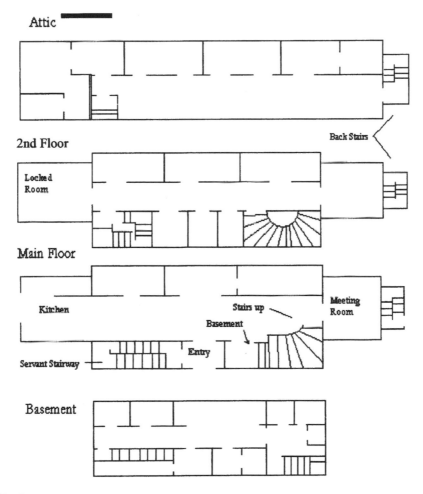

Attic

2nd Floor

Back Stairs

Locked
Room

Main Floor

Kitchen

Stairs up

Meeting
Room

Basement

Servant Stairway

Entry

Basement

Fusion.

GHOSTS

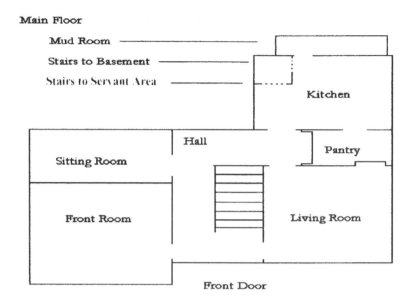

Main Floor

Mud Room

Stairs to Basement

Stairs to Servant Area

Kitchen

Hall

Sitting Room

Pantry

Front Room

Living Room

Front Door

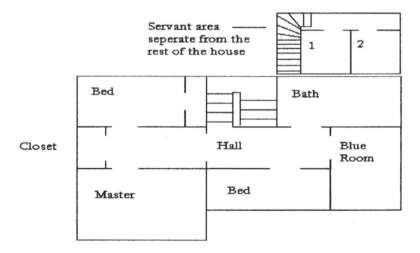

Second Floor

Servant area
seperate from the
rest of the house

1   2

Bed

Bath

Closet

Hall

Blue
Room

Master

Bed

Farmhouse.

1

INTRODUCTION TO THE
PROPERTY — FUSION 2005

It all started very innocently, as these things usually do. We had just finished an in-depth ghost investigation for the City of Mississauga and were packing up our equipment when a maintenance supervisor looked at me and said "I know of a place with a reputation of being haunted. Interested?"

I was tired and looking forward to going home and getting some much-needed sleep, but as a paranormal investigator I just couldn't say no.

I asked Paul and John if they wanted to go, and without hesitation they both said yes. We piled into my car and I followed the supervisor to the house. We drove in silence. Paul was sitting in the back seat; I could see his disappointment in the rearview mirror each time we drove past a coffee shop. John just stared out the window.

John looked at me as I drove and said, "There is a door that is open — it's broken."

"Where, at the house?" I asked.

"I sense a door that has been broken and is now insecure." Then he went back to looking out the window.

Fusion.

John Perrone is a gifted clairvoyant who has worked with us on most of our investigations for the past fifteen years.

We pulled off the main road and stopped in front of a large gate. We watched as the maintenance supervisor slid the gate open and waved for us to proceed. I pulled my car past his truck and drove into the darkness. My car's headlights illuminated the long tree-lined driveway. Ahead of us we could see the house growing out of the night's black cloak. We parked in the circular drive in front of the mansion and just sat there, quietly taking in the view. I was the first to step out of the car. The night was cold and I pulled my jacket tighter as the dampness moved inland from the lake. Even though there were several people there with me, I had this overpowering sense of loneliness and isolation. I looked at Paul and John, both staring up at this massive structure, to see if their faces would give away what they might be feeling. The only person whose facial expression read like a book was the supervisor; it was obvious he didn't want to be here. I quickly started snapping photos of the house with my digital camera as John and the supervisor discussed the mansion. Paul started off to explore the property.

"Rick!" Paul called out in a voice that was both hushed and urgent. I turned and saw him at the path just past the side of the building. It was difficult to see him as Paul typically wears all black and tonight was no exception. I started walking toward him when I became confused; my pace slowed as my mind tried to figure out what I was looking at. The black shape that I thought was Paul was someone or something else, as I *now* saw Paul standing just beyond this shadow. Whatever it was now stood directly between Paul and I. It half turned and moved across the path at an impossible speed to a small twenty-centimetre-round maple tree and vanished. I was caught completely off guard, evident from my camera hanging unused by my side. Paul moved forward and we looked in the direction of where the shadow had vanished, but there nothing, not a shred of evidence that it had been there. We both tried to talk at once. Paul had been behind it and described it as an all-white luminescent figure of a person; I had seen it as a black shadow in human form. This confused us; we were both looking at the same image, but seeing it completely differently, as if what we were looking were a photonegative. We were both excited about the encounter and kept going over the event as we joined John and the supervisor. I was sure the supervisor was on the verge of bolting from the property. It was then and there that we made a rule — no one went anywhere on the property alone. I explained to the supervisor what we had encountered, that the need for the rule was common, and that we saw apparitions all the time. This seemed to calm him a bit, but of course, for his sake, I had lied. I couldn't help but look over my shoulder. I had a bad feeling in the pit of my stomach. The way this thing had gotten so close between my brother and I, without making a sound, made me very uncomfortable.

The four of us walked around the house; the rear of the mansion was even more spectacular as it had a high patio that overlooked a sprawling yard leading to Lake Ontario and Joshua Creek one hundred metres away. It was there that we discovered the sliding patio door, recently broken and opened five centimetres. We examined the door and the supervisor determined that a bar inside had stopped whoever had tried to break in. I looked at John. "Well, there's your broken door!"

John just nodded.

We continued around to the front of the house, where we stood and talked about its history for a few minutes. Paul and I kept looking back to the spot where we had seen the figure. I knew that I had to come back and do a proper investigation here as this place had instantly captured my interest. We were about to say good night when I caught a movement from above; it was ever so slight, more of a subtle light change than anything. I looked up at the house and there in the second-floor window was a person looking down at us. "Look!" I yelled and everyone looked up.

The person jumped back out of sight.

"There was a person looking out that window!" I said, excited.

They probably thought I was overtired. Then a hand appeared, pulling back the blind, and a head and a shoulder came into view. It jumped back again, the blind swaying. This time we all saw it.

The supervisor automatically believed that someone had broken into the house. He looked to the front porch and saw the lights on the security alarm pad were all green. He pulled out his cellphone but had trouble finding a signal. After trying for a few moments he was successful and placed a call to security to respond to the property immediately. We waited. Paul tried the front door, but found it locked, so he joined us in the driveway as we watched the window.

Security arrived with the keys and we rushed the house, threw open the front door and stormed onto the main floor. I quickly turned to my right, looking for a way up to the second floor. I slid to a stop on the dust-covered tiled floor. "Guys," I called out, looking up. The group quickly headed to where I was standing, also looking up. The window where we had seen this person was positioned above the grand staircase in three metres of open air space. There was no floor for a person to stand on and no way to even get close to this window. We stood there very quietly for a few minutes, allowing this discovery to sink in. I looked at the security officer, "I don't think you have an intruder here." I whispered to him.

He rushed us out of the house, reset the alarm, and sped off. After ten months of chasing ghosts all over Mississauga, this place became the place I needed to investigate because in a matter of thirty minutes we had encountered more activity, visual spirit activity, than in all the other locations combined. This truly was a

The shadow person was seen looking out of this window at Fusion.

significant haunted location. I really needed to have a cigarette. I lit up as we were making plans to come back for an investigation. The supervisor made it clear that he wouldn't be returning, but would make all the necessary arrangements with security to let us in the next time we wanted to come and do some work here. I dropped my cigarette to the ground to put it out, and in a matter of seconds from when it left my hand to fall to the dirt path, it vanished. I wasn't sure at first and thought my eyes were playing tricks on me, but the others had also noticed. Without a word, everyone took two steps back and we scanned the ground for the white, filtered stick with the glowing orange ember, but there was nothing. It was somehow gone. "No wind at all, that's strange!" Paul said. We stood there for a couple of minutes, looking everywhere, even searching several impossible places without any success. We finally gave up and walked back to our vehicles. I could see the supervisor was extremely uncomfortable, so we quickly made plans for our return and with that we said our goodbyes and left the property.

As we drove home everyone was excited about what we had encountered and couldn't wait to go back; we were already making plans.

"There are many secrets hidden there," John stated.

2

FIRST VISIT —
INTERIOR, AFTERNOON

When Paul, John Perrone, and I arrived, security opened the main door to allow us access, and left shortly thereafter. This behaviour struck me as odd, as most people have a natural curiosity about what we do. This gentleman certainly didn't seem to want to hang around. We toured the house, starting in the basement, which was a jumble of rooms, some with high-security card-reader sensors on their doors from the last company to inhabit this place. The rooms were littered with old computer cables, communication trunk lines, power boxes, and a variety of dead bugs and spiderwebs. We made our way back up to the main floor and could quickly see the massive changes done to the house by Hydro while the house was in their possession; a kitchenette was at one end of the house, a boardroom at the other. It was nice to see, however, that several of the original fireplaces still remained. The second floor had several rooms, which had the odd chair or metal desk in them. We located the servant stairwell and went up to the attic, a massive space that had been divided into several offices. I stopped to take in the spectacular view of the property from one of the windows. It was like a dream. As I looked down across the rolling, manicured lawn to the lake and inlet to Joshua Creek, several white-tailed deer moved along the water's edge. It was difficult to believe this was the same place where I had been the other night. It looked peaceful and inviting — a thing of beauty. However, as the sun sank and night came, the property underwent a dramatic change; the grounds became watchful and somehow sinister. The house felt lonely, almost as if it was mourning a great loss. What mysteries would we find here? What still dwelled in this place?

The three of us made our way back to the main floor and set up a table and chair for John in the boardroom. He would try to obtain a sense of what might be going on in the house with regards to spirits and their history, and with any luck we would learn how to proceed with our investigation and what, if any, challenges we would face here.

John sensed a woman and that she had suffered great loss here; he felt that she was once the matriarch of the house. "She still resides here," he told us. "This was a place of music and parties. There was a lot of happiness, but also sorrow here."

Our first point of business was to discover who this woman was and how she was connected to the house and property. If she was trying to hold her family together this was more than likely her home at one time. Could it have been her we saw at the window on our first visit here? Not likely, as both Paul and I agreed the figure at the window seemed to be that of a male. And what of the strange creature we had encountered by the side of the house; what was it and how did it fit into the history of this place?

Paul and John explored the house as I wandered the floors and took baseline readings of electromagnetic fields, temperature, humidity, and ambient sounds. I also looked for anomalous frequencies and, because Hydro had used the building for experiments, I scanned for low-level radiation, of which none was found. I found this strange as there should have been some background radiation at the very least, but there was nothing at all. I also created a map of the interior of the building, indicating lights, switches, vents, windows that could open, machinery, and air flow.

Even though the house was silent I had the distinct feeling of being watched. Nothing menacing, simply a quiet curiosity. People sometimes ask me, "If you take baseline readings in a haunted house, how can you tell they are normal and you aren't recording an anomaly at that time?"

Baseline readings are recorded initially and all other readings are compared to them. Had an anomaly been recorded on the first visit, with the reading now completely different on the second visit, then that would provide the investigator something interesting to look at. If subsequent readings are found to be identical to the second visit, then the reading from the first visit would, of course, be considered the anomaly.

I came down to the main floor and met Paul and John, who were talking in the centre room. I had just arrived when we heard heavy walking coming from above us. We all hurried upstairs to see what was making the sounds, but as we arrived, the sounds stopped. We couldn't determine where they had come from as the second floor is completely carpeted and walking sounds should not have been audible. There were definitely strange things going on here.

It was getting late and we had run out of time. Unfortunately, we hadn't had the chance to tour the coach house to the east end of the property. We decided to call it a day.

3

FIRST INVESTIGATION

We wandered through the darkened house, turning on lights as we proceeded slowly, listening for anything out of the ordinary. We knew something was here haunting this place and I half expected to turn a corner and run into whatever it was. Paul and I moved our equipment in and set up one audio/video camera on the main floor, one on the second floor, along with the infrared in the basement. Once everything was in place we set them to record and left the main house, making our way over to the coach house to place an audio/video camera on the main floor.

The coach house was quite large; a great room on the main floor that was once an area big enough to park three cars, sat completely empty, flanked by large power boxes. At each end were stairs leading up to the sleeping areas now converted to office space, on the second floor. To the south of the room was a kitchen, bathroom, office, and large closet. To the north were the stairs to the basement, the mechanical room, and bathroom. After a tour of the servant areas on the second floor we decided to head out and explore the grounds.

Coach house.

"LET ME OUT OF HERE!"
(EVP EXCERPT FROM SURVEILLANCE TAPE)

Paul and I walked west around to the rear of the main house, while John and Chris headed east to the far edge of the mansion. Paul and I heard something moving ahead of us. We cautiously followed the sounds leading us toward the stairs to the lower yard, the light beams from our flashlights cutting a path for our advance. The sounds retreated from us, leading down the stone stairs. We followed, quickening our pace.

Meanwhile, on the far side of the house, Chris moved back toward the front of the mansion, thinking that we were still in the area. John paused at the side glass doors, which gave him a commanding view of the main floor; he stood watching as a man crossed the floor in the far meeting room. He couldn't determine any specific details because of the distance and low lighting, but he knew it was a man. Chris came back and met up with John again.

Paul and I reached the bottom of the stairs and the sounds were dead ahead of us, moving along the interlocking stone. They were loud and clear, but we could see nothing. The basement light poured out onto the patio and still we could not see the source of what was retreating from us, and then it was gone, or it had simply stopped moving and was hiding there in plain sight. We crossed the patio and ascended the steps to the east side of the house, meeting up with Chris and John. John told us what he had seen.

We entered the house and investigated the meeting room, then the rest of the building. We found nothing out of place and came down the stairs to the ground floor. Chris was first and as he turned, he looked back down the hall to the glass doors that John had previously been looking through. He stopped, frozen in terror, as two luminescent figures stood beyond the glass looking back at him. He motioned for us to look, but they vanished before we had a chance. Chris was unnerved by what he had seen and was very uncomfortable remaining on the site for the rest of the evening.

The investigation was brief, but very successful as both John and Chris had seen visual spirit activity. We would have to wait a few days for Paul to analyze the recorded information and see if anything was captured. We conducted a final tour of both the main house and coach house, collecting our equipment as we did so. John again sensed this mystery woman, stating that she was full of sorrow and that she was on the second floor of the mansion, but there was nothing further from her.

"DANNY BOY"
(EVP EXCERPT FROM SURVEILLANCE TAPE)

Paul called me the next day and told me we had captured a few EVPs; it was his opinion that a child and male spirit were at the house, and we should plan for our next visit. The main EVP was that of a male calling for a child who was named Danny, specifically "Danny boy."

Although John and Chris both reported seeing phenomena in the house, the camera failed to capture anything other than audio occurrences.

4

HISTORICAL RESEARCH

Paul and I embarked on a journey of hundreds of hours of research into the countless mysteries of this house and property. In the early stages we had received many pages of false information, which caused great confusion and conflict. It puzzled us as to why some people wanted the history of this family to remain lost. At first I thought it was an error during the collection and compilation of the data, but then I looked at some of the sources; these same people were very meticulous in compiling historic information for the City about its people and properties. They led us to believe the house had changed hands eight times, when in fact there have only been three owners, the City being one of them.

First mystery solved: the historians from Mississauga had told us a tale of a family who had bought the property and built the mansion and, with an air of mystery, refused to live there, instead fleeing the home and leaving it to be later purchased by the Gairdner family. We later found this was not the case at all.

What's in a name? Gairdner Estate, Fusion Centre … if we followed proper etiquette the place should have been named for its builder and first owner, as are all old rural properties. If that custom had been followed, then the Bell Estate would have been its rightful name.

The City of Mississauga has identified the property as holding an archaeological interest. It was the Ojibwa who hunted, fished, and lived in this area from 1700 to the late 1800s. They became known as the Mississauga Band. The Mississauga Band always maintained a deep relationship with nature, as it was their belief that all things had a spirit. They would sprinkle tobacco as an offering to spirits that dwelt in these sacred places. To them, there was no difference between natural and supernatural. They believed that at death the shadow or shade of the deceased would remain to haunt the living, while the person's soul would travel to the land of souls. They would practise *Jeebanahkawin*, a feast for the dead, offering food and tobacco. They had a great respect for all things and believed in "The Great Spirit" (*Keche-munedoo*) and an "Evil Spirit" (*Mahje-munedoo*) and a great host of other spirits that kept watch over everyday events.

The land comprises forty-eight acres and was purchased in 1937 by Charles Powell Bell, a prominent defense attorney from the Roberson family farm, which at the time was owned by the Abbs family. The construction of his estate began immediately and in August 1938, Charles moved his wife Kathleen and his young family into their new home, which faced Lake Ontario and the mouth of Joshua Creek.

The house was built on a steep slope, which makes it look taller by one storey on the southern exposure. It is a two-and-a-half-storey building with a gabled roof and is punctured by three third-storey dormers on the north side and four gables on the south side. Originally extending out from the wings of the house were two one-storey white structures, built on top of cement block foundations, which were demolished in 1983.

The coach house once had three large garage bay doors, which have been removed and replaced with windows and converted to office space, along with the living quarters upstairs. There is another garage buried deep in the brush at the southeast end of the property, also with living space above. To the west was once a large in-ground pool and a pump house.

The pool has been long since buried; only a corner of its blue ceramic edge protruding from the ground tells of its location, and the pump house has been badly damaged. Ontario Hydro made massive changes to the structure during their tenure.

Within three months Charles was dead; he died on November 7, 1938, at the age of thirty and was buried at Mount Pleasant Cemetery. Incidentally, Charles had lost his last court battle trying to have George Little acquitted of shooting at Police Chief Inspector John Chisholm in a gun battle.

In 1918 James Gairdner married Norma Ecclestone Smith; they had five children. In 1936 Mrs. Gairdner died of a heart attack. James Gairdner married Charles's widow, Kathleen Harding Bell,

Outline of the pool.

in 1941, and the two families joined together, living at the property on Lakeshore, which became known as Gairloch, a Gaelic word meaning "short lake" and chosen for the property by James Gairdner.

Following a severe attack of arthritis in 1959, James took up oil painting and built a large art studio on the west side of the property.

James and Kathleen divorced in 1960 and James bought a large estate up the road in Oakville, built in 1922 by Colonel William McKendrick. He moved his studio from its location on the Fusion property to his new home. The studio can be seen today as his property and studio were willed to the City of Oakville and are now known as Gairloch Gardens, although in actuality should be known as Gairloch #2, as the original property in Mississauga was first to be named Gairloch.

It was interesting to note that, upon our visit to Gairloch Gardens, the property was devoid of James Gairdner's art, even though he had painted over four hundred canvases. His beloved studio is now being used as a tuck shop.

Although Paul and I spoke to several people who worked there, we heard conflicting stories about the main house and gallery. Most stated that neither were haunted, however, a few said that when they stayed there overnight they had heard things they couldn't explain. Whether it is or isn't haunted could not be confirmed, as our request for an investigation was turned down.

As Paul pointed out, the gallery was designed to specifically match and compliment the mansion in Mississauga; the exterior held the same lines as the old mansion and would have fit in as an aesthetically pleasing addition to the property. Once inside, you can get a feeling of how the original house may have looked prior to Hydro's renovation of the mansion and coach house.

In 1961 Kathleen sold the property to Ontario Hydro and moved to Toronto. The property became the base for Ontario

Hydro/Canadian Fusion Fuels Project. Ontario Hydro also purchased the Robertson farm of sixty acres in 1970.

Kathleen died in 1991 and now rests beside her first husband, Charles, at Mount Pleasant Cemetery.

James died in 1977 in Barbados. His funeral service was held in his beloved art studio; several sources have stated that his ashes were spread outside his gallery, however, this could not be confirmed.

The City of Mississauga acquired the property from Ontario Hydro in 1997.

As we researched the family's background we discovered a problem common to families pre 1970, prior to the women's rights movement of the 1960s. Kathleen had been married twice, first to Charles and then to James. James had been married three times. While conducting our research we found that women did not have their own identity during this time period, instead carrying the husband's complete name; the only distinction they had that separated them from their husband was the title "Mrs." When searching news or archival files on Kathleen, for example, there rarely was information other than Mrs. Charles Bell, or Mrs. James Gairdner; we then had to try to separate James's three wives by dates before we could determine which wife the article referred to. We pressed on.

5

INTERVIEWS

It is important to hear from those who, while conducting their duties, had a paranormal experience while on the property; it allows us to gain a slight glimpse into what might be occurring at the site. These interviews become even more important when different people, who have never met, describe similar incidents and details.

THE GROUNDSKEEPERS

"We arrived early and parked the work truck between the mansion and coach house. There had been a storm the previous night and we had to pick up branches and do a general cleanup of the grounds. Banks of fog moved inland from the lake, making everything wet and cold. We didn't really want to be there so we quickly went to work, hoping we could get it finished and leave. I worked my way to the back of the property, picking up branches as I went. I lost sight of my partner as I went behind the house and he was working the front yard.

"I had just thrown some sticks into a pile when something moved to my left; I just caught it in my peripheral vision. When I turned to see what it was, there was nothing there. I continued working when, ahead of me, the fog swirled and something black moved toward me. At first I thought it was a person; it looked like a person except it was all black, like a shadow. It had a head and shoulders, arms and legs, but there were no features. It approached me and directly behind it was another one. It didn't have eyes, but I could feel it looking at me. I turned and ran for the truck. I was sure I was screaming for Frank, but honestly, my heart was pounding so strongly in my ears, I couldn't hear a thing. When I was nearing the truck I saw Frank also running toward it. I could see he was yelling something at me. We jumped into the cab, Frank gunned the engine and sped off with my door still hanging open. We drove for a while in silence and then after we had finally calmed down I told him what I had seen; and he told me that he had seen something similar near the pump house."

THE GROUNDSKEEPERS II

"It was a very beautiful morning. The sun was bright and warm and we had arrived to do some work on the property. Joe offloaded the ride-on lawn mower from the trailer and I started pruning the shrubs and hedges at the side of the house. I had always heard stories about this place, but it always just seemed like a wonderful place to me; you just didn't know what you might see here, from wonderful owls to white-tailed deer or foxes. I came to the back steps of the house and looked out over the property to the lake; something caught my eye. It looked like two people were down by the water. I climbed a few stairs to get a better look; it was two people, a man and a young woman, they were wearing wedding attire, old-fashioned wedding attire. She had on a wedding dress with a veil and train and he wore a black top hat and tails, a high white collar, and a bow tie. They were arm in arm; it was a very strange sight. I looked to my left and saw Joe sitting on his mower, stopped, watching the couple as well. I looked back at them and as a breeze came up off of the lake, the couple seemed to just disintegrate, vanishing in the wind. Joe yelled to me, 'We're going!'

"I hurried back to the truck, loaded our equipment, and left. It took me some time to realize that I must have just seen two ghosts."

SECURITY

Ron said that security has responded to countless alarms at the site, the majority being internal intrusion detection. All have been false, meaning that there was never a reason found for the activation. He recounted times when security arrived to find lights on when they were not on during previous checks on the property. On occasion, patrol personnel have chased odd noises though the house, but have never found anyone trespassing. The worst was when there was an alarm in the coach house; staff really didn't want to go there. Everyone hated going into that building because the feelings of being watched and unwelcome were very oppressive. On one occasion the system went off-line and security was dispatched to investigate. The patrol officer found that the main alarm control box had melted into a pile of unrecognizable goop; the alarm company was called in to look at the system. The technician could not explain how a low-voltage system could generate enough heat to completely destroy the components and outer box.

SECURITY II

"Oh that place, I hate going there. We get calls of internal-motion detection alarms, no perimeter alarms, just *inside* the house. I will never forget driving up to the front of the house and using the car's spotlight to scan the grounds. As I passed the spotlight near the east corner of the house a shadow of a man was cast on the wall of the house, but there was no one there, let alone someone standing between my spotlight and the wall. I drove back to the road and called for backup and waited for them to arrive before I went back in there. Of course, I didn't mention this to my fellow workers, but I found it to be absolutely terrifying."

SECURITY III

"I had heard a great deal of stories about this place so, while on my rounds, I decided to go have a look and log a patrol of the property. It was late when I pulled up in front of the house. I got out of my car and, as I turned towards the house, movement caught the corner of my eye. I turned and watched two black shadows walking across the path between the main house and the coach house, heading toward Lakeshore. They were the shape of a person, but it was almost as if they were black voids; they were darker than the background and you couldn't see through them. I had never felt fear like I did at that moment. Now I try to stay away from that place, or at least wait for my partner to show up before I go in."

SECURITY IV

"I don't really believe in any of this stuff, I have heard the stories and find it quite amusing. I've been out to that property many times for patrols and checking on security alarms. I will admit that I do get the feeling of being watched when I go out there at night, but I have never seen anything strange."

TRADES

Eric worked on the property a few years ago. He was hired to do some painting on the exterior of the buildings on the property. He had set up his ladder and was painting window shutters on the northeast corner of the front of the main house. He was working when he had a strange feeling, as if being watched. He looked down from his ladder and spotted a dark shadow of a person cast across the lawn next to a tree by the side of the house. He said it took him a few moments to figure out that there was no one there casting the shadow. Within a minute or two the shadow took a couple of steps and faded away. It took Eric almost twenty minutes to gather the nerve to come down off his ladder, pack up, and get out of there. He refused to return to finish the job.

I was very intrigued by some of the accounts that I had received, especially regarding the dark shadow people, as these resembled what Paul and I had witnessed that first visit to the property. The potential for us to capture activity at the mansion looked extremely promising; we were already recording EVP there. It would seem that John Perrone was right, that there were a number of mysteries there and the team and I were very excited about this project.

We met and started planning for our next investigation, I wanted to invite the team from Peterborough out and get their opinion on the house. I contacted Dee Freedman and she agreed to come out along with Krystal Leigh.

I made arrangements with Chris for access; Chris was reluctant about coming out because of his last experience at the house, but decided he would attend. The arrangements were set, and I couldn't wait to return. There was a strange pull on me to go back — this was beyond my normal curiosity. Looking back now I see that it was borderline obsession; something was drawing me back to this place.

6

SECOND INVESTIGATION

GET OUT OF THIS HOUSE OR I'LL ...!"
(EVP EXCERPT FROM SURVEILLANCE TAPE)

W e arrived at the house. I stepped from my car into the freshly fallen snow. The sun was just sinking below the horizon and I felt a chill. This was more than the icy wind coming up from the lake, but I still pulled my coat tighter, hoping to ward it off. Chris opened the door to the house and as I could see the team enter the main house as I pulled the equipment from the car trunk. Paul came over and helped unload the car and moved everything into the mansion. It wasn't much warmer in the mansion as the heat was set to a bare minimum to keep the pipes from freezing. The house was dark and very quiet and we all went to work quickly setting up our equipment. Paul placed some target items in view of our surveillance equipment; the idea was that specific items can tempt the spirits to move or tamper with them and sometimes, depending on the item, they may elicit an emotional response. One item was a doll. The rule we follow is that when toys are used in a location where children's spirits are believed to dwell, the toy, once deployed, cannot be removed as we feel this may be seen as cruel, or some type of punishment. At the end of each investigation all target items are photographed and inspected to see if there was interaction, after which they are collected and removed, all with the exception of the doll, which will be left in the hallway on the second floor where Paul placed it.

The five of us moved outside and headed over to the coach house where Paul, Chris, and I set up audio/video surveillance on the first floor. The camera stood near the door to the kitchen and had a commanding view of the main floor all the way to the front door, the basement stairs, and the stairs to the second floor. It could not, however, see the second set of stairs to the second floor, which were directly behind the camera. All of the lights were on and the house was empty and quiet.

The camera recorded the three of us leaving via the main front door, where we met Dee and Krystal outside. The audio portion of the tape captured Chris slamming the front door shut. Immediately after the door closed there was the distant sound of heavy walking, coming up from the basement stairs. The camera failed to capture an image of what was making the sounds, but they continued toward the door and then, as if someone were kicking the wall or door, there came loud banging and a sigh. A moment later the walking became louder as it directly approached the camera. A male voice was recorded saying "Excuse me!" and then all fell silent.

Thirty minutes went by and then the lights started to turn off in sections, a section would go out and then come back on and the next section would go out and then come on again, and so on.

Paul, Chris, Krystal, and I entered the coach house while Dee waited just outside the front door due to asthma (a mould warning was clearly posted). As they searched the house, I changed the tape in the surveillance system by the kitchen, Paul checked all the electrical panels, but was unable to find any timing system or anything else that would explain the lights coming on and off, there was nothing except simple standard light switches. I joined the search and found a hidden hatch under some empty boxes in a closet near the main floor bathroom. We opened the hatch revealing a wall of cobwebs, spiders, and centipedes. We used a broom to move the bugs and webs aside. Paul lowered himself into the pit and scanned the pitch-blackness with his flashlight. "There's stuff down here!" he called up.

"What stuff?" I inquired.

"It's hard to see, not a lot of space between the ground and the floor above. There are a lot of pipes in here!" His light went black and something skirted across his arm. I lowered a spotlight down to him.

"There's an old trunk and a very old baby carriage. I have no idea how they even got them down here."

"Is there anything in the trunk?" I asked him.

A baby carriage was found in the coach house crawl space.

"Give me a minute," he said as he struggled to reach the trunk. "It's empty, looks like it's from the nineteen-twenties or early thirties."

I handed him the digital camera and he snapped several shots.

"All right, let me out of here!" he said, handing Chris the camera and spotlight. Chris backed up so that Paul could hoist himself out of the crawl space.

I called the museum manager to advise her of the artifacts that we had discovered and their exact location.

Krystal had made her way to the front door and was holding it open and speaking with Dee about what we had found. I rechecked the surveillance camera and then all of us left the coach house.

The five of us walked around the coach house into the far yard and before long we were all experiencing oppressive feelings and an overwhelming sense of being watched. As we came around to the southern end of the building, the feelings intensified. We moved to the east side of the property where the boundary was marked with a chain-link fence with a forest beyond. It is this area that evoked the darkest feelings; most of our photographs that were taken in this location would not turn out. It was almost unbearable to remain in that area and some of us wanted to turn back. Dee stopped and focused on the southeast corner of the coach house. "Someone is buried here," she said. She wasn't sure if the body lay under the structure or just near its edge. We paused to examine our options — there weren't many at the moment other than to note the location. We couldn't bear these feelings any longer and the five of us headed back toward the front of the main house. As we did, the oppressive atmosphere started to fade away.

As we crossed the parking area between the two houses, movement caught Krystal's eye and we were all drawn to the far field in the northeast, where we saw a large human-shaped shadow pass between the trees, only to vanish. We stood there watching and waiting, but whatever it was had disappeared, and it seemed, at least for the moment, that it wasn't about to return. We continued off toward the mansion, all looking back over our shoulders, half expecting, half fearing it may again be there ... closer.

It was time for a break; we entered the house and went to the meeting room on the main floor to have a hot drink and a snack.

We collected our thoughts and discussed the different areas of the property and how, depending on where you were on this property, you could traverse the entire spectrum of emotions. The house held anger on the first floor, fear on the second, a mix of sorrow and joy in the attic, and a playful curiosity in the basement. Outside was simply oppressiveness and foreboding. Everyone noticed that there was a strong difference between what haunted the house and coach house and what roamed the grounds; there was something very strange about the entities outside, but we just couldn't put our finger on what it was. Whatever they were, we definitely took notice and would exercise a very strict caution out there. I faded away from the group's conversation, remembering our first night here and the entity on the path and how easy it was for it to stealth its way to within a few metres of my brother and I. Sure, spirits did this sort of thing all the time, but this presence did it in such an intentional way, it was clear to me it meant to send us a message, perhaps a warning, as it moved into position, and when it was ready, it made sure that we saw. In that instant the message was delivered. There was a genuine fear, although during an investigation I have to take such emotions and find a safe place in the recesses of my brain to bury them. For how long, I couldn't tell, however, I knew that fear could be a funny thing and would try to bubble back to the surface, sliding along the natural grooves of the brain; you either had to deal with it or it would pull you down into an abyss where you became nothing but fearful of everything and ghost investigations could no longer be conducted. That wasn't an option.

GHOSTS

"THEY'RE COMING UP! THEY'RE COMING UP!"
(EXCERPT FROM SURVEILLANCE TAPE)

Paul was checking the first-floor camera; I asked Dee if she would come upstairs with me. We started up and I called to Paul, telling him that we were going upstairs.

On the second floor there was a surveillance camera, which was looking east from the westerly room past the main stairs, east down the hall. The tape in the camera recorded me calling to Paul, "We are going upstairs!" An unknown male voice yelled out in a panic, "They're coming up! They're coming up!" Then two black shadows peeled themselves off the stairwell banister and blurred past the camera, going into the room at the top of the stairs adjacent to the camera. A moment later Dee and I appeared at the top of the stairs; we looked at the camera, turned left, and headed down the hall.

If working in a haunted house isn't nerve-racking enough, it's when you examine the surveillance tapes and discover that these spirits came within metres and sometimes centimetres of you. Some were angry and, even though you were not aware of it at that moment, they were yelling at you and even uttering threats. It sure makes you pause the very next time you enter the house and find yourself standing on a darkened floor.

"KATHLEEN"
(EVP EXCERPT FROM SURVEILLANCE TAPE)

A few hours later we all met at the bottom of the main stairs. Everyone sat on a step and we discussed the house. I thought I had heard something, but wasn't quite sure what. It became clearer that it was singing — a woman singing. I looked at the others to see if they were hearing it as well, but there was no indication that anyone else was hearing this. So, like a conductor, I started waving my hands to the rhythm of her singing. They looked at me and, as if they had been hearing it subconsciously all along, they all quickly acknowledged the music.

"Someone is singing," Paul stated, looking up the stairway.

Krystal smiled. "That's incredible."

Dee and Chris quietly listened.

She sang for a few more minutes and then fell silent.

We were absolutely delighted by the singing woman experience, and whatever fears we had seemed to have been washed away. The mood seemed lighter, and even Chris appeared to feel better about being in the house, more relaxed.

We split up and decided to conduct a final tour of the main house before it was time to pack up and head home.

Dee and Krystal had made their way down the east stairway and were exploring the basement when Paul, Chris, and I came down the main stairs to the basement. It was very dark and it was strange that the lights were off; we were following the beam of our flashlight to a closed door that led into the great room. Paul led the way, pulling the door open. Dee and Krystal heard us and froze, as they did not know it was us entering, only that something had just pulled the door open and was coming to where they were, and we didn't know that they were there either. The five of us virtually walked into each other in the dark. Then, out of nowhere, came giggling, wholehearted laughter from a small child. It brought a smile to my face. The smile was brief, replaced by a wince of pain as the grasp of a hand clamped down on my shoulder like a steel trap. I looked back at Chris who, in terror, had grabbed me. I shook him loose and calmed him. Then the small child was gone, leaving us with nothing but silence. We waited a few minutes and then the five of us returned to the main floor.

I looked at Paul and smiled, remembering the EVP from our first investigation, "Guess you're right about a child being here. What was his name?"

"Danny! Danny Boy," he said.

We all went outside to allow the surveillance equipment to do its job. We find that the best results are achieved when the house is empty. In places that have more than one spirit we normally capture our best EVPs when no one is around and the spirits have an opportunity to talk to each other; it would seem this house was no exception.

It was becoming early morning and we were about to pack up our equipment and conclude our investigation. I went up to the attic to do a final check of the house. When I traversed the servant stairway, something didn't seem right, so I stopped on the second-floor landing and just stood there for a few moments, trying to figure out what it was. Then it came to me: the handrails in this stairway were polished and there was not a speck of dust. I dragged the sleeve of my black coat over the railing and then looked at it — nothing. I lowered myself to look between the banister rungs — still no dust. This was extremely odd in a house that had been shut down for almost ten years; if there was one thing that this house had no shortage of, it would be dust and dirt and spiderwebs. Someone was still doing their job here. It would seem that the mundane continued into the next life as well.

A couple of days later Paul advised me to come and hear what we had captured on tape. I arrived at his house and settled in to review what he had found.

It was a man calling Danny Boy, a woman calling for Henry, and Captain. It seemed the man was giving direction to the child as he would order him to "Come here" and "Get back."

I was truly amazed as we could recognize two different and distinct voices and it now seemed we had two names and a nickname from the house, this should assist in our research.

7

THIRD INVESTIGATION

"HENRY, KEEP QUIET! GET BACK."
(EVP EXCERPT FROM SURVEILLANCE TAPE)

We entered the main house and found it extremely quiet. We conducted a quick tour as we normally did, set up our surveillance equipment, and then met on the main floor.

We stepped out into the night and immediately felt a heavy, oppressive feeling around us.

The feeling affected each of us. We couldn't determine if it was coming from any one direction; it just seemed to envelop us.

Paul wanted to do more work in the coach house; he wanted to learn more about the spirit there as we didn't really know much about him, other than the impression that he seemed angry, yet somehow polite, as was revealed by our last visit's surveillance tapes. The problem we were having was that whoever was haunting the coach house was alone and therefore had no one to talk to. As we found in the main house and at other locations, when there is more than one spirit, they will talk and use names, and we are able to gain this intelligence through the collection of EVPs. We wanted to move away from this oppressive feeling, so we decided that shifting indoors might be better. We walked to the coach house where security had left the door open for us and we entered.

John P., Chris, Paul, and I went to the kitchen area.

John stopped briefly, sensing. "He's young, in his twenties," he said, then addressed the spirit. "We are not here to harm you, we just wish to communicate with you." John paused, then smiled. "He says he is sleeping!"

Paul looked at John. "So wake him up!"

Chris had some concern with the whole idea, "No, let him sleep, don't wake him."

"Have you been sleeping long?"

John sensed a reply. "Yes."

"Where are you sleeping? Can you show me?"

John sensed another reply. "Yes."

With that, John walked off past the kitchen to a back room and pulled his pendulum from his pocket. "Please show me."

The pendulum started to swing southeast and John followed the direction across the room until he reached the wall. The pendulum stopped moving and just hung there. "Is this where you are?"

John sensed a reply. "Yes."

"Well, it would seem that whoever this person was, he is buried here."

"That's at the far end of the crawl space," Paul said.

"We can have a look for anything that might be obvious, but we aren't digging for a body here," I told them.

Paul readied himself to go down into the crawl space and have a look around.

John paused, and then looked at us. "He wants a toy."

"How about a dog?" Paul asked.

John waited. "He would love that."

Paul retrieved a small, stuffed dog from his kit and handed it to Chris. We opened the hatch and Paul lowered himself into the

Paul emerges from the crawl space in the coach house.

hole. Chris handed him a spotlight. As we waited around the open hatch, Paul's head came into view and he looked up at us. "It's possible that something is buried there, the ground is just earth and there is a depression at the end of the space," he reported.

"I don't think it's a good idea. First of all, we don't have permission to dig, and second, there's a mould hazard. Once you start disturbing the ground the spores are going to become dangerous," I said decisively.

"Yes, let him sleep," Chris stated.

Chris handed the stuffed dog to Paul, who placed it a few metres into the space and took a photo of its placement, face up. We helped Paul out of the crawl space and closed the hatch.

Chris and I retrieved the project box from my car and brought it to the coach house. Paul opened it and we set up a camera near the kitchen.

We headed back to the main house to change the surveillance tapes. As we arrived on the second floor Paul called to me, "The doll — it's not here!"

I placed a new tape into the machine and pushed "record" then stood up, looking down the hall toward Paul. "What do you mean? I just saw it earlier."

"Well, it's not here."

We searched the floor but found no sign of the doll.

The house was quiet and we spent almost two hours going from room to room throughout the house, everyone keeping an eye out for this doll. It was never found.

We stopped on the main floor. John sensed that this house was once a place of grand parties and extravagant events; it was also a place of music. On the darker side, there were some deeply hidden mysteries here. That inspired me, as I truly enjoy digging into mysteries.

"I see a lot of people. They are all dressed in tuxedoes and ball gowns and everyone is wearing masks, very delicate masks of feathers and of fur to cover the eyes. Very strange party," John explained.

"Strange how?" I asked.

"I'm not sure, it just feels strange."

"Halloween?"

"No, not Halloween, just a gathering," John stated, pausing.

"There is a fear here. They fear us. Wherever we are in the house, they will move away to another part of the house to try and avoid us," John said.

"Any idea why?" I asked.

"They are just afraid of us! But they are watching," John replied.

A few hours later we started packing up the equipment in the main house and loading everything into my van. We went into the coach house to retrieve our surveillance equipment. John stood near the kitchen. "Check the dog," he said.

Paul pulled up the hatch and we peered into the crawl space

with the spotlight. The dog was still there. "Hold on, that dog was face up when I left it!" Paul stated.

He looked again, and it was now definitely face down. "Are you sure?" I asked.

"Yes, I took a picture," he told us.

I pulled the digital camera from my pocket and started skimming through the photos. There it was, the picture of the dog Paul had taken, laying in the dirt face up. How this stuffed dog had flipped over defied explanation. I took another photo and we closed the hatch.

"Maybe he's showing us that he's buried face down!" Chris said.

We collected our equipment and the four of us left the site.

Over the next few days as Paul reviewed the surveillance tapes he couldn't believe what had been recorded. He called me right away.

"We have dozens of EVPs on tape, but most importantly we've recorded four names and one nickname," he told me. Electronic voice phenomena was great, but I was more excited over capturing names because this information would be very important as we started to look into the history of this property, and hopefully tied these names to this estate's past. From the main floor system we had recorded the names Henry and Danny, more specifically "Danny Boy." From the second-floor camera were the names Kathleen and Tonya and again we got someone who was referred to as Captain. I was thrilled by one EVP more than any other, Kathleen, for this name was linked to the owner of the house. Could this mean that she was there in spirit? Was this the person John talked about sensing? It made a lot of sense. The EVP that referenced Captain was a bigger mystery because, as Paul pointed out, it could be either a military person or someone who had sailed a boat. It could also be the title given to the head of the servants, the person who manages all the other staff for an estate of this size, and we knew that there was an army of servants that had lived and worked on the estate, according to a descendant of Mr. James Gairdner.

For a moment I thought that this reference may have been to James Gairdner because he was an avid sailor and yachtsman, but dismissed it because he held the rank of major in the First World War and would not have accepted a nickname below his earned rank.

Tonya seemed to be another child who played with Danny Boy, either she was older or had some authority because we found on the EVPs that people would direct Henry to look out for Danny and Danny appeared to be a great burden of responsibility to Henry, whereas Tonya seemed to be able to come and go as she pleased.

Paul was concerned about the spirit in the coach house. We might never learn his name if he had no one to talk to.

8

FILM SHOOT

I was contacted by Darrin LaPointe, a director from Ignition-Horizon Pictures. He was aware of what I was doing on the property and wanted to meet me to discuss doing a film on the Searcher Group while we conducted our investigation. After some negotiation we came to an agreement. It seemed like an intriguing project, and I was very interested in his technical crew as most of them were self-proclaimed skeptics. It was a fantastic opportunity that would allow me to observe several skeptics interacting on the property and, more importantly, allow me access to their opinions during and after the shoot.

After negotiations with the City, permission was granted to film on the grounds only, with entry to the structures restricted due to insurance requirements.

I had to wonder how his crew would fare spending twelve to fourteen hours outside with the dark entities we had encountered several times, and further, how my team would hold up, as there would be no safe haven since we would all have to remain outside for the entire duration of the shoot.

Paul, Amanda, and I arrived at the gate. John Burnell was already set up and providing security for the site. We pulled in and parked in the lot closest to the road, as this would be where our base camp would be staged. Scott McClelland, our host, arrived, as did Darrin and his crew. His technicians situated a portable generator and work station to charge batteries and provide extra power if we required it.

I started going through my kit, checking my equipment and replacing all the batteries. Amanda headed out to take photos of the cast and crew.

Darrin called for me, saying that the first thing he wanted to do was have a complete tour of the property before we lost the sun, so several of us headed off toward the house.

We discussed where I wanted to set up a couple of cameras for surveillance: one facing the main house, specifically the window through which I had first seen the figure looking out, and the infrared camera at the back of the house, looking toward the lake. He was satisfied by the tour and headed off to talk to his crew and shoot a couple of interviews.

The interviews went well, but then power and technical problems started cropping up with every piece of equipment. The camera I had set up in the front of the house failed, but in a way that John Mullan, our technical specialist, could not explain, as he checked each component and each worked fine. It just wouldn't record when facing the house.

Camera operator Justin was mystified while running a series of tests to prepare his equipment. He warmed up his camera and ran bars and tone, as you would normally see when a television station goes off the air. He turned the camera off, but the images persisted in his viewfinder. He pushed his auxiliary "off" switch, but still the images remained. In frustration, he pulled the battery unit from the pack; his camera continued to operate for several minutes. Inexplicably, the camera seemed to be pulling energy out of thin air. Impossible, he thought.

We were setting up a surveillance camera that faced the front of the house when Paul yelled out, "There's something standing there!" and pointing to the path at the side of the house. This was the same spot in which we had encountered the strange entity on our first visit to the property.

I pulled my gauss meter from my jacket pocket and walked toward the path with a camera in front of me and another following. I led with the meter, scanning the immediate area for electromagnetic fields. It was picking up nothing at all until we arrived at the side of the house. My meter picked up seven milligauss, and as it started to register, the cameraman in front of me began to have some technical difficulty and his camera's lights dimmed slowly to black. I moved the meter from side to side and up and down, trying to determine the size of the electromagnetic field. Just as quickly as it had come, the field was gone, my meter fell to zero, and as it did so, the camera lights blazed back to life, almost blinding me.

Sound operator Grant stood with several members of the team, discussing something that they had seen that had passed the second-floor window when he felt a hand grab his leg. Even though he knew it was a hand, he tried to rationalize it by looking for a vine, branch, or wire from his equipment. He found it was none of those things and became frightened; however, he kept working the shoot.

We worked on into the night, trying to cope with the increasing electrical and technical problems — then things started to become really strange and unnerving.

During the shoot we had pushed these dark entities to the limit. Maybe there were too many of us present for them to feel comfortable or maybe they had just had enough.

During all of the visits to the property, violent actions were never experienced, it now seemed that they, whatever they were, wanted us to leave. They seemed to be targeting the weakest links in our cast and crew.

Paul, Darrin, and I were talking, making plans for our next scene, while camera 2 moved around us, filming. I looked at the cameraman and he seemed pale. I didn't care about the shot, so I looked directly at him and asked if he was okay. He said he was fine and just kept filming.

Darrin and Paul started to walk toward the camp and as I turned to look at them I heard a muffled fall behind me. I turned to find the cameraman lying on the ground, semi-conscious. "Man down!" I yelled, which brought everyone running.

It took a few minutes to get him to his feet. He had no recollection of what had happened. He went back to camp and sat there for an hour or so. Not long after, Scott began to feel ill and felt that he could no longer continue. Darrin gave him a blanket and let Scott rest in his van parked at base camp, where he quickly fell asleep. When one of the crew went to check on him, he called for us to come quickly. As we arrived, he pointed out tiny handprints on the van's passenger window, as if a child had stood there, leaning on the window, looking in at Scott sleeping. The handprints were small, only ten centimetres from the tip of the middle finger to the end of the palm; handprints that were too small to belong to anyone present that night.

Amanda was testing the parabolic microphone, a device we use to boost even the slightest sounds so we can hear them more clearly. She started wandering the parking lot, just east of the base camp, when she heard noises in the bushes ahead and to her right. She moved in to see what it was and came face to face with a shadow person. They both froze, yet, as frightened as she was, she felt that it was not a threat but rather that it was curious about her. She turned and made her way back to where the rest of the team was keeping an eye on this dark creature. It moved quickly and ran toward the bush and vanished in a blur before reaching them.

Paul looked at Darrin and me. "We need to bring in the psychic and see what she has to say," he said.

Darrin sent his personal assistant to call for Michele to join us at the camp. She arrived a few minutes later.

"We want to give you a tour of this property. Let us know if you sense anything, okay?" I explained.

She was drawn to the coach house and we all walked off across the lawn toward it. Upon reaching it, we stopped briefly in front and then headed around to the rear. As we neared the back, Michele stopped and looked at one of the windows. I looked at it as well but saw nothing.

"There is a young man there. He died a violent death. He is acting very pleasant, but it is only an act; he wants me to come in and help him, but I know he will hurt me if he gets the chance!"

She was talking about the lone spirit in the coach house. "What else do you sense about him?" I asked her.

"Nothing, just that he pretends to be polite, but is dangerous." And with that we were off and heading back towards the camp.

We met up with Scott. He looked pale, but wanted to continue, so I redirected the group toward the house.

Paul, Michele, Scott, Darrin, the camera crew, and myself were walking up the front driveway to the house. We were a few metres from the fountain when Michele stopped. She looked towards the house wide-eyed. "The little girl is saying something."

We all stopped and waited, listening.

"She says go back, danger!"

All around us, in a tight circle, we could hear the sound of feet on the ground, trampling gravel, twigs, and leaves, moving quickly, and yet, looking around us, nothing was moving. I saw the faces of the crew, panic was starting to show. "Be calm," I told them.

It was then that we heard a loud, hollow thud and Michele's leg flew forward. I moved around Scott to grab her arm to steady her. Something unseen had just kicked her savagely in the back of her calf.

"Someone just kicked me!" she complained.

There was no wind. The air was cold and still and all around us were sounds and whispers; we needed to pull back to safety.

Michele was pushed and that signalled the retreat. We all turned and quickly made our way back to our camp.

The bruise on Michele's calf was deep purple and immediate. It was time to take a break and rethink our strategy.

John Burnell had volunteered to provide security for the shoot and positioned his van just inside the front gate. He set up a small folding table, chair, laptop computer, and settled in for a long night.

It was just after midnight when John got up to stretch his legs and walk around. He was about six metres away from his post when he felt something strange, like electricity. The hair on his arms and the back of his neck stood up on end and then he heard the giggle of a small child right next to him — that of a young girl. Startled, he rushed toward the house where we were filming to tell us what had happened and to show me the goosebumps on his arms, but, more importantly, he wanted to be near other people at that moment. John had always maintained that he was an open-minded skeptic about the supernatural, but now admits what he experienced was unnerving and unexplainable.

I checked with Scott and Michele — they were ready to go and wanted to continue. I signalled to Darrin and he immediately had his film crew around us.

Paul, Scott, Michele, and I stood in front of the house. Michele looked at me. "I sense those shadow energies are all around us. They are circling us."

We couldn't see them, but we could hear them moving around us, shuffling along the ground, and through the leaves. We could feel the electricity in the air.

"DON'T DO THAT!"
(EVP EXCERPT FROM CAMERA 1)

I looked over at Grant as he stood there holding the microphone, panic growing on his face. "Be calm, it's okay," I told him. I could only imagine what he must have been hearing through that microphone. I really had no idea if we *were* okay, I just didn't want anyone to panic. He focused on his task and we all stood our ground.

"Did you hear that?" Michele asked us.

"Hear what?" I asked.

"Don't do that!"

"Don't do what?" I inquired.

"I just heard a man say 'don't do that.'"

We had no idea what we should or shouldn't be doing, so we pressed on.

It wouldn't be for a few days after the shoot that Darrin located the EVP from his sound recordings for me, and confirmed that an unknown voice did in fact say "Don't do that."

Paul, Darrin, Scott, Michele, and I, with the film crew in tow, thought we would head over to the pool to see if Michele could psychically pick up on anything there. The pool, which had been buried, was about eighteen metres directly north of our position at the west side of the house and the path to the pool was bordered by a single row of hedges. We started out on the short walk and then something happened that had never happened to us on this property before — we became disoriented and ended up one hundred metres west of the pool. I just looked at Paul and shook my head. It took him a moment to orient himself, "Impossible!" he said out loud. I just couldn't understand how we became lost on such a short walk with so many landmarks to guide us.

Michele looked at us and said, "They are laughing!"

A quiet laughter could be heard on the breeze. The idea of going to the pool was abandoned and we headed back to the base camp.

GHOSTS

When we arrived at the base camp, everyone split up, looking for coffee, a snack, or a place to sit quietly and take a much-needed rest. Darrin and I talked about what we were going to do next and then he was off, hunting down his personal assistant. I grabbed a bottle of water and stepped into the shadow next to a clump of trees, looking off toward the coach house. Paul joined me, coffee in hand. We were going over some of the night's events when something caught our attention. A solid black figure walked out of the trees and crossed the field next to the coach house before quickly disappearing into the brush south of the house. We stood there in silence. "So where's the cameraman?" he asked.

I looked over my shoulder, back to the camp. "They're on break."

"That's three times tonight! We need to move the infrared camera to watch this spot," Paul suggested.

I called John Mullan and Darrin and told them of our plan to pull the camera from the rear of the house and set it up so that it could monitor the coach house and surrounding area.

Later in the evening, the camera, facing the coach house, caught a brief, strange movement; the coach house has a light that comes on and goes off as it gets too hot, then cools and comes back on again. It was when this light had gone off that a dark shadow moved, ever so slightly, in the background. When the light came on, the shadow was more pronounced. We were shocked to see the shadow move a few centimetres to its left so it would be away from the light. When the light went out, the shadow had vanished.

The shoot was finished; it had been a very long night. I met up with Darrin at the base camp; he seemed pleased at how everything had gone. He went over the exciting events of the evening as we packed up our equipment. We said our thank-yous and goodbyes as the cast and crew pulled out of the parking lot. The sun was up now and Darrin, Amanda, and I were the only people left on the site. Darrin wanted to conduct a final walk-through to make sure we had collected all of our extension cords and hadn't left a mess anywhere. The three of us walked up the driveway to the house, then headed west around to the back of the property. As we came around the corner we ran into a man wearing walking shorts. He also sported a cane, a gray handlebar mustache, and a brimmed hat. He was very distinguished-looking. He had come up the stairs from the back of the house and was walking directly west. We all said good morning and he continued on his way. As we neared the back of the house, we all turned in unison without saying a word and looked west. There was no one there. It was at that moment that it dawned on all of us that something was strange about that man. Where had he come from? To the east of the property is about two kilometres of petrol refinery land, not the most ideal area for a stroll, not to mention that it was very early and quite cold for walking shorts ... and where had he gone? Directly west was more forest and a high chain-link fence. He looked as real as any one of us, but remains a mystery to the three of us to this day.

TECHNICAL PROBLEMS

Afterwards, we reflected on all the technical problems we faced during the shoot.

Darrin had supplied six high-quality, one-million-candle-power spotlights for the film shoot; every time the cast or crew took them near the house and the east side of the property, these lights would fail. Each time they failed they would be collected and taken back to the base camp, where John Mullan was waiting to provide needed battery charges. John had just sent out two lights and was astonished to have them back only ten minutes later because the manufacturer rated the lights for ninety minutes of continuous use. He hooked them up to his battery analyzer, which told him they were fully charged. When he pushed the switch, they blazed to life. He tested them in several different ways and each time they showed as being fully charged; he was at a loss as to what to do with them. Shortly thereafter, another two came back from the field and again he found the same results. This time he sent one of the units back out, the other he turned on, placing it on his work bench to monitor its performance.

It wasn't long before they ran out of usable spotlights. Darrin came back to the base camp to find out what was going on.

"John, we need some lights; is there nothing we can do?" Darrin asked, looking rather frustrated.

"They're fully charged! I can't very well charge them any more than they are. This one was brought back twenty minutes ago and it's been on since."

"How long did you charge it for?"

"I didn't, your crew brought it back to me and told me it was dead, I just turned it on and laid it here. It's been working perfectly ever since."

Darrin shut the production down temporarily and called a meeting with John and myself. The only solution was to move to the west side of the property and hope that the equipment wouldn't be affected as badly.

Not only were we having a high level of problems with our lights and equipment, but we also noticed cellphones would rarely work while we were on the property, even though the transmission tower wasn't that far away. Cellular phones would work when the user first arrived and usually continued to work for about fifteen to twenty minutes, and then they would fail to maintain a signal.

It was interesting to note that security complained that their mobile radio reception was poor as well.

John Mullan subscribes to the National Institute of Standards and Technology and wears a watch that receives a national time signal that automatically adjusts to the official time via this signal. After midnight each night his watch will search for this signal and will make six attempts to receive this signal, approximately every hour. John spent the entire night outside on the property during the shoot, the sky was clear; however, during the entire reception window from midnight to 6:00 a.m. his watch was unable to synchronize.

Now with the film shoot behind us, I turned my attention back to the investigation of this magnificent property and the spirits there. I called Chris and told him I wanted to go back as soon as possible and, as usual, he was kind enough to make the arrangements with security.

9

FOURTH INVESTIGATION

I couldn't help but find it fascinating that even though my team knew that the house was haunted, the majority of them, along with those whom I interviewed, found the property around the house to be the object of their concern. Many had a greater fear of what lurked outside in the darkness and even though they understood that there were spirits in the house, they preferred to be inside rather than exposed on the grounds. It was true some had had experiences with the dark shadows, however, a great deal of my team had not. They could not clearly express why they had this fear on the property; they just had a feeling that it was safer indoors. When we did go outside to investigate, we normally did so in teams. Although this didn't alleviate the feelings of dread, it did allow the members enough confidence to wander the grounds.

Darrin LaPointe had expressed his desire to come back to the property and have a chance to see the inside of the house; he was welcomed as a member of our team and invited to come out with us.

Darrin, Paul, and I took our equipment to the kitchen. We had decided to use this area as our command post as there was a large, old desk and a couple of chairs in the room. As we came in and put our boxes on the floor, Paul noticed something in the dust on the desk. We gathered around this imprint, which was clearly the handprint of a small child.

Upon closer examination it was clear that the print was new, as there was no accumulation of dust inside the print. I checked with our contact only to find out that no one had been in the house since our last visit and a child wouldn't have been in this house for many years. Paul guessed by the size of the print that it most likely belonged to a child between five and seven years old. The end of the palm to the tip of the middle finger measured ten centimetres. Darrin quickly reminded us of the small handprints we had discovered on the passenger window of the minivan during the film shoot. Was this evidence that the spirit of a child roamed the house and property? What tragedy had befallen this child and why were they haunting this place?

A child's handprint on the desk.

Paul wanted to try some lighting control experiments with the video surveillance equipment. As I set up the camera equipment on the second floor at the west end of the floor, facing east, Paul brought up a lamp and placed it in the centre of the hall. He plugged the lamp in and the bulb lit up the hall briefly, then the light quickly turned a dull orangey colour. He called me to come over and look at the lamp. I walked over and noticed the strange colour and that the air around the lamp was defused, almost foggy, and was spreading out from the lamp and filling the hall.

"What's wrong with it?" I asked him.

"Nothing, it worked at home, there's a sixty-watt bulb in it."

Darrin stepped into the doorway to the hall to see what we were talking about, and within a moment the light became a brighter white and the strange glow and fog were gone.

"That's not normal," Darrin said out loud, checking the lamp.

"Nothing seems normal in this place," I told him, turning my attention back to the camera equipment.

As we were setting up surveillance throughout the house, Paul was busy placing target items in view of the cameras. Some of the items were stringers of bells. The extra items were left in a box in the basement, next to one of our cameras. On the second floor he laid out a square of baby powder in the doorway of the most easterly room, a room that in the past had yielded paranormal activity. He applied the powder to make it difficult to enter or exit the room without disturbing it. Once everything was set, we headed downstairs and outside to investigate the grounds.

As usual we felt eyes on us as soon as we stepped out on the front stair; we lingered at the front of the house for a few minutes until Paul suggested we go to the coach house.

We entered the coach house and Paul immediately wanted to have a look in the crawl space; he felt he had to check to see if the stuffed dog was still there and have a closer look at the trunk and carriage. He wondered if there might be other, smaller artifacts down there that he had missed, something that might lend a clue to this lone spirit in the servant quarters.

We opened the hatch and when Paul lowered himself into the hole, the first thing he saw was the dog in its proper place, and then his light failed. I lowered my light down to him and in a moment it, too, failed. "Give me another light!" he called up.

I didn't have another one with me, they were all back at our command post in the kitchen of the main house.

We just stood there looking at each other in silence for a couple of seconds.

I left Darrin and Paul working in the crawl space and headed back to the main house to retrieve another flashlight. As I came out of the coach house and started crossing the field, my pace slowed as I suddenly felt unseen eyes watching me. I stopped and turned in a circle, looking into the darkness and expecting to see something looking back. I had broken my number-one rule: "No one goes anywhere on this property alone." The feeling of being scrutinized intensified and as I picked up my pace toward the front door, something moved to my left, near the tree where a shadow figure had been seen several times, but I didn't look and just kept moving. I rushed into the house, allowing the front door to slam behind me. I took a moment to breathe, then retrieved two lights. I approached the front door, hesitating. I pushed it open and stepped out onto the front stoop, looking toward the tree. There was nothing there. I scanned the grounds between the coach house and my position. The sense of being watched returned, followed by an uneasy feeling. As I started walking in the direction of the coach house, a branch snapped to my right; I peered through the darkness, saw nothing, then heard another snap. I stopped and turned toward the sound, shining my light at it, and still nothing was there. I hurried to where the others were waiting for me.

Darrin looked at me, "What took you so long?"

"Nothing!" I said, and handed him the flashlight.

With nothing more to be found in the crawl space, we helped Paul out of the hole and had a tour of the upper floor of the coach house. We heard the odd noise, but put it down to the furnace and headed back to the main house.

The three of us started in the basement, working our way through the house, changing surveillance tapes as we went. As we arrived on the second floor, Paul and Darrin went down the hall as I pulled the tape. Paul called me, excited. Darrin started filming with his camcorder. I rushed down to join them, "What is it?" I called ahead, arriving at the end room.

"There in the powder, look, it's a footprint!" Paul said, pointing at it.

I looked down and there it was, a perfect, albeit strange, print in the powder, which hadn't been there previously. It looked like a slipper, size eight or eight-and-a-half. The strange

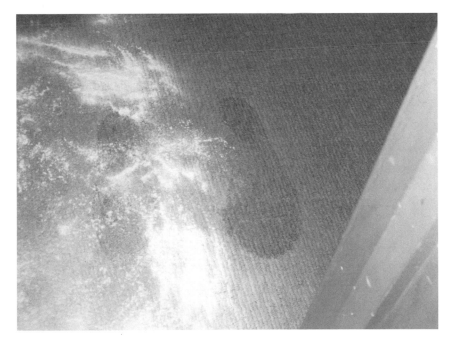

Footprint in the powder on the second floor.

77

thing was that even though the outline of the slipper's sole was quite defined, we could clearly see five toe prints inside the outline of the slipper. Paul jumped over the powder into the room, and as he landed, a cold breeze came from nowhere and the temperature of the room plummeted, followed by popping sounds like static from inside the room. As quickly as it had come, it was gone. The temperature returned to normal and there were no further sounds. Paul moved to the left side of the room and demonstrated how the person to whom the slipper belonged may have stood. They would have had to have hidden behind the wall and leaned out to peer down the hall from the doorway.

I had to wonder if this was Kathleen's footprint. Was she keeping an eye on us?

After photographing the print, we made our way to the main floor. I wanted to test my theory that by causing an emotional situation in a haunted house it may be possible to elicit a response from the entity present. We had captured several EVPs where the name Danny Boy was called out by another spirit in the house. If the spirit of this person was actually here and the person calling him had close ties to him, I should be able to provoke them into some type of action. I placed my portable stereo on the main floor, right at the bottom of the open stairway to the second floor. I inserted a pre-recorded CD and pushed "play." Judy Garland started to sing "Danny Boy," filling the house with music for the first time in many, many years. I felt moved as I stood in the hall listening as the music echoed through the empty rooms. It was a strange feeling, as if the house had missed this, a feeling somewhere between sorrow and joy. As the song ended I walked back to the kitchen to join Paul and Darrin, as I did so Glenn Miller's instrumental version of "Oh Danny Boy" started to play. Paul and Darrin seemed to be uplifted by the music. The three of us talked about how we felt as the music filled the house; we all experienced strange emotions as if a calmness fell over us, and at that moment we felt as if everything was all right. The music ended and all was quiet. We just sat there listening.

"COME HERE, DANNY BOY."
(EXCERPT FROM SURVEILLANCE TAPE)

The silence was shattered by two men talking loudly on the main floor near the front door. Startled, we thought it might have been security returning to check on us. The three of us responded, leaving the kitchen and heading down the long hall toward the front door. There was no one there. We arrived at the door but found nothing; it was locked. Paul went to the stairs and I stepped out into the front yard. No one was found. All three of us heard two men speaking, almost arguing, and yet none of us could tell what they were saying.

It was days later, when Paul had reviewed all of our audio and video, that he found several EVPs. The first was of men talking in a low, indistinguishable mumble, and from the basement the bells from the box of surplus next to the camera were being played with. The camera itself was jostled and moved slightly.

The investigations seemed to be going well, but slowly. I wanted to bump it up a notch.

10

PLANNING FOR THE
NEXT INVESTIGATION

I have been developing a theory over the past several years of what I have termed "The Memory Bubble." It is where I believe spirits exist. The bubble is a self-devised reality, created by the entity out of the fabric of their personal memories and emotions, as if living in a waking dream. These bubbles exist on the fringe of our own reality and, during specific situations, may collide with and merge ever so briefly with our reality and therefore allow us to experience things we define as "supernatural." These bubbles resonate at very low frequencies, all of which are beyond our perception until something happens to allow our reality and their reality to momentarily synchronize. It was during the development of this theory that I felt I should be able to create a device that would open a window and allow me to look into other realities. I had to investigate how plausible it was to build such a device and what frequencies I would need to access for this to work. I understood that with the detection of particles and anti-particles appearing from out of nowhere — only to disappear again — that the science of quantum physics was now showing us that what we perceived as empty space was not empty at all.. The thought was that these particles could be moving through alternate realities, and could only be observed as they passed into our specific reality. Science has expressed the likelihood that there are a multitude of alternate realities around us.

During my research, I came across several articles that piqued my curiosity; they seemed to point me in a direction that said everything that exists is connected, and the component that bound each and every thing were specific frequencies.

The first article was from Stanford University, entitled "The Singing Sun." The article explains that, according to Kenneth R. Lang, our sun is playing a secret melody that causes parts of the globe to beat like a heart.

The second article was carried by the BBC news service and is entitled "Listen to Your DNA," wherein Susan Alexjander, along with Doctor David Deamer, explores the sounds of human DNA and Ms. Alexjander actually turns these sounds into music. It seems everything has a frequency and we just have to find new methods of access them.

This gave me great hope that I should be able to locate those frequencies that would allow me to access the reality of life after death. The biggest problem I had to overcome was discovering which frequencies, or band of frequencies, would allow me to do this. I turned my focus to dreams and dream states, as I felt there was a hidden clue to the answer I was looking for. Although there is a great deal of data about dreams, solid information about what dreams are and why we have them eludes modern science. They could very well be a pseudo-reality.

As we enter a dream state we are fully capable of experiencing all physical and emotional sensations, such as pleasure, pain, joy, and fear. This to me demonstrates how our minds can create all the emotions and feelings, without the need for a physical body. The dream state operates at a very low frequency, normally between the Delta brainwave pattern of 0.1 to four hertz, and during REM sleep, where vivid dreams and nightmares occur, between the Alpha brainwave pattern of eight to thirteen hertz. If these frequencies were within the range of what I was looking for, then I needed to substantiate them.

When a psychic makes contact with spirit energy there is an unexplainable change within their brainwave patterns. Where they are awake, conscious, walking around, and talking, their normal brainwave patterns should be within the Beta frequency range (fourteen to thirty hertz). However, when they establish contact, their brainwave patterns fall into the low Theta frequency range (four to seven hertz), and on rare occasions into the high Delta frequency range (0.5 to 3.5 hertz). It is interesting to note that Theta is the dominant brainwave pattern in children under four years old.

I believe this change in brainwave frequency allows psychics to perceive and communicate with energies that exist on the fringes of our perceived reality. The psychic normally receives information and images in their mind from the spirit or spirits present.

EXPERIMENT 1:
WELL-DOCUMENTED PSYCHIC (UNITED STATES)

The subject entered the hospital and met the doctor prior to testing. The subject was taken to a lab where he was attached to various machines, one being an electroencephalogram or EEG. Over the next few hours, various tests were conducted that showed the subject to be within normal conditions. The next phase began by having several people brought into the room, one at a time, to be read by the psychic; people whom the subject had never met before and knew nothing about. The subject conducted readings for each of the people, with astonishingly accurate details regarding people who were close to them and had died. The most

83

interesting part of the experiment was that while each reading was taking place, the EEG showed higher activity in the right side of the brain of the subject. Even though the subject was fully awake and active, the EEG showed theta, borderline delta, brain-wave patterns. After each reading, the subject's brainwave patterns would return to normal. This activity could not be explained by the doctor.

EXPERIMENT 2:
WELL-DOCUMENTED PSYCHIC (JAPAN)

The subject entered the hospital and met the staff and doctors. She was connected to a wide array of equipment and tested to ensure that her physical and mental conditions were within normal parameters (which they were). The subject was then introduced to a person whom she had never met before and commenced her reading of this person. The subject's left brain shut down and the right brain went into theta, borderline delta, wave patterns.

If these two psychics show normal brainwave patterns at all times, with the exception of when they engage in readings (during which their brainwave patterns change drastically, allowing them to establish an open line of communication with the other side), then the switch must be located within the right side of the brain. If we look at all the available data, we should be able to isolate the frequency range.

I wanted to develop a device that would not only find and isolate the location of a spirit, but also establish open, constant, and consistent communication with them. My first step was to try to discover what it was that I was looking for, so that when I found it, I would recognize it. I approached a senior lab technician who worked out of a government institution that I was associated with, and gave him a basic description of what I was looking for. Within thirty minutes he had rigged a simulator, using a frequency analyzer to replicate what the bottom end of the hertz spectrum would sound like. As he queued in the frequencies, he hit one in particular, and I told him to stop. I had heard this sound before. This was the same annoying sound I had heard on several of my control tapes that were made in the house that contained paranormal activity, and it fell directly within the parameters of the data I had collected.

I believed that I had the frequencies for my theory to work, but I felt there was some part of the equation missing. I had to find the proper way to introduce these frequencies into the environment for it to be successful. My research brought me to a finding made years ago by Gariaev and Poponin at the Russian Academy of Sciences in Moscow, termed as the DNA Phantom Effect. The unexpected discovery was made while measuring vibration modes of DNA using a laser photon correlation spectrometer. They noted purely by accident that when the DNA sample was removed and the laser was fired again an image remained, like a phantom resonating out of time and space. It was a few years later that they came to believe that they had discovered mechanisms of subtle energy phenomena, or subtle energy fields, and is coupled with electromagnetic fields. Dr. Poponin feels that the DNA phantom effect is "[a] subtle energy manifestation in which direct human influence is not involved," and sees it applying to "the physical theory of consciousness."

The experiments concluded that the phantom effect had unusually long lifetimes and could exist in both stationary and slow-propagating forms. Further excitement came in the new hypothesis that the phantom effect is a manifestation of a previously overlooked physical substructure. The substructure can be excited by energies close to zero energy. This effect may explain the phantom leaf effect and the phantom limb phenomena. The phantom leaf effect refers to Kirlian photography, where in 1939, Semyon Kirlian began photographic experiments using electricity and found by using this method that he could capture the aura or corona of organic objects. The most impressive were a set of photographs of a leaf: the first was the leaf with its aura, and in the second when the top of the leaf was cut away and re-photographed, the image showed the half leaf, however, the entire aura was visible as if the leaf remembered how it should appear. This inspired me to pursue my theory of the memory matrix of spirits.

The other point of interest related to these phenomena is what is known as sensory phantoms, wherein people who have had a limb or body part amputated report the feeling of pain or other sensations coming directly from the missing limb. According to Dr. Jack W. Tsao, approximately 90 percent of amputees experience these types of sensations. I firmly believe this to be not only related to the DNA phantom effect, but also to the Kirlian phantom leaf observations, and fit directly with my theory of the memory matrix.

After carefully examining the information that I had compiled, I felt that I knew how to proceed. What I needed to do now was figure out how to create the experiment and find the right place to execute it. The location wouldn't be a problem as I was currently investigating one of Canada's most haunted properties. To resolve the hard question of how to conduct the experiment, I took my data to John Mullan and Lester Hickman and told them what I wanted to do. We worked out the details and theorized that in order for it to work we had to create a standing wave. Mr. Hickman drew up the plans to demonstrate how I could produce the correct frequencies within the field and listed the necessary equipment I would need. I already owned most of the equipment required, and the rest could be borrowed.

I assembled the equipment, but the entire experiment gave me pause. I postponed the project while I tried to calculate the possible impact of what I was about to try. On one hand I felt like an explorer about to journey into the unknown, as nothing like this had ever been attempted before. There was no research, no notes, and no background on which to base the possible outcome.

On the other hand, I felt fear; was it fear of the unknown or fear of something else? I couldn't be sure. After a great deal of discussion with people in the field of life-after-death research, I decided to proceed with the experiment.

I set up access to an old servants' residence, which was the hub of a multiple haunting that was the focus of my first book, *Overshadows*, back in 2003.

I assembled the equipment according to the diagrams provided by Mr. Hickman, measuring out the placement of my speakers to ensure the standing wave would fill the room. I had enough time to check the wiring before two of my three observers arrived. Two of them were team members who were working on the investigation. We waited on the third, who was a self-proclaimed skeptic, and it was his opinion that I would be most interested in after the experiment was concluded.

I set up my Sony camcorder and tape recorder and while we waited we talked about the investigation until our skeptic came to the back door. The house was completely empty; there was no furniture, so they found a corner and sat down on the floor while I started the equipment. I switched on the frequency generator and quickly found the desired frequency, then set the camcorder and tape deck to record. We sat quietly for fifteen minutes until I could see they were becoming restless and I began to wonder if my theory was wrong. It was at this point that we started to experience auditory phenomena — the floors began to creak and we were hearing hollow sounds of walking and whispering coming from all directions. The room started to get hot, but I didn't have any environmental equipment on hand with which I could measure the difference, so I couldn't tell how hot it was or what the exact change might be. The air started to change, as if black soot were floating upon it. From out of nowhere shadows started to move; shadows of people skirting along the walls. Panic erupted in the room and my skeptic friend jumped to his feet and headed for the back door. I cut the power to the equipment and someone threw the switch to the large, overhead light and the room looked normal again. I ran for the back door and chased down my friend, who was halfway across the parking lot. I finally caught up with him and he was extremely upset, too upset to return to the house; he just wanted to go home. I returned to find my teammates standing outside, waiting for me to return. It seemed that my theory and experiment were truly a success; the three of us were excited and were talking over each other about what each of us had experienced. The whole event was exciting and a bit terrifying as well. We packed up the equipment and called it a night.

I was completely aware of other theoretical work that had been brought forth by Vic Tandy regarding the possibility that infrasound could cause people to hallucinate paranormal phenomena, as well as Dr. Michael Persinger's theory that electromagnetic waves could trigger the strange feelings and sensations attributed to ghostly phenomena. Could I have proved them right? Did my machine cause the four of us to hallucinate the entire event? Was my theory a bust?

It wasn't until the next day that we had the opportunity to sit down and review the audio and video tapes that had been set up in the house to monitor the experiment. We watched as the camcorder tape played on my TV. First came audio sounds: floors creaking, walking, although you can clearly see the four of us sitting still. Then the whispers started, like crackling static, along with the odd word. This was very exciting, but then you could see the air change, as if the room were filling with dark particles and then, as quickly as it had started, it was over, the lights came on and we were running out of the house. It was no hallucination; four independent observers and electronic equipment cannot falsely see and hear the same things simultaneously. My theory had worked; it truly was an incredible discovery.

After all these years, here I was about to test this theory for a second time, with more observers and better surveillance equipment. I had to wonder what might lie ahead.

I sat down with Paul and started to work out a tactical plan for conducting this type of experiment at Fusion. We knew that for the experiment to work, the spirits had to be in close proximity to the test field that the apparatus would generate. This was going to be our biggest challenge, as the house was quite large and, judging from our previous investigations, the inhabiting spirits seemed to be afraid of us, meaning that wherever we were in the house, they would surely be elsewhere. We devised a plan where we would "squeeze" the house, forcing the spirits to the spot where we wanted them to be. We would arrive ahead of the rest of the team and set up the equipment in the basement, as this location gave us the largest open area. We would place our surveillance equipment and then we would leave the house and wait for everyone else to arrive. Once the team was assembled outside we would move, as a group, directly up the servant stairway to the attic. Once there, we would leave two members behind and proceed down to the second floor, leaving a member there and then so on down to the main floor. If the spirits moved away from us, as they had in the past, then logically they should end up in the basement. It would be at that point that the participants of the experiment would go downstairs and start the experiment. We had our plan, now we just had to make it work.

I called a few select members of the technical team and discussed our plan. I wanted to be sure that I hadn't missed anything and was, as always, looking for other opinions and input. It was during one of these discussions that I was drawn into a conversation about what we were trying to do. The last comment that was made chilled me to the bone. "We need to be careful of what we are doing. Remember the Last Judgment (End of Days), where all those who live and all those who have lived stand upon the earth at the same time. Essentially, that's what you are describing, or at least that's what I'm hearing!"

It made me pause, as this was the first reference made to what I was basically trying to do. It was not, however, my intention to do such a thing, but rather to have a glimpse into another reality. It made me realize that the two things could very well be the same, depending on point of view. I left our meeting feeling torn about running this experiment in hopes of recreating the situation that had revealed itself on the first trial of this test back in 1995. Its fantastic results could possibly bring us that much closer to touching and understanding the other side of our physical existence. Who knew what possibilities lay ahead? But on the other hand, who knew what would happen when that door was thrown open? I certainly didn't. I remembered the first time we ran the experiment and what had happened. Knowing the horrible things that had occurred there and what haunted that place told me that if there were no lasting ill effects, and there didn't seem to be, then the experiment in a fairly passive environment like Fusion should be safe. I needed to know for sure and at that moment decided to proceed with my plans to conduct the experiment.

11

FIFTH INVESTIGATION

"ANNA RITA, COME HERE."
(EVP EXCERPT FROM SURVEILLANCE TAPE)

W e had obtained authorization to continue our investigative work at the site; the team would assemble at 7:30 p.m. Paul, Amanda, Darrin, and I would arrive early to meet with security and go over some of the past events. When Amanda and I arrived at the gate, Paul was already waiting. He was excited and handed me a pair of binoculars, "The second-floor window, something small and white keeps passing the window." I looked through the binoculars, focusing my attention on the window above the stairway, but I couldn't see anything at the time.

"I saw it twice, it was small, like a child. It didn't have any features," Paul told me.

"Let's go up to the house," I said and walked around, pulling the gate open. We drove to the front of the house and parked, where the three of us looked up at the window and waited for a few minutes, but nothing happened.

"Let's have a walk around and check out the property before security arrives," I suggested.

It was cold and snow was falling lightly, which made the stone stairs at the rear of the house hazardous. We circled the house and checked the coach house; everything seemed to be in order. We waited in front of the mansion for Darrin and security to arrive; it was starting to get dark.

It was in the early stages of our investigation that Paul had introduced a doll as a target item, as we believed a child's spirit was present and we had hoped there would be interaction between the doll and the spirit.

Note: 2006 — Back in Our Third Investigation

Security opened the door and we conducted our walk-through to ensure the house was empty and had not been vandalized. Everything looked as we had left it from our previous visit. The one exception was the doll that Paul had left on the second-floor hallway, which was missing. We searched the house extensively, but the doll, unfortunately, could not be found. We asked security to check and see if other people had been in the house, but were informed that no one had been there since our last investigation.

2008 — Present Day

Paul, Amanda, and I arrived at the house and toured the property; everything looked in order. We settled on the step near the front door, waiting for security to arrive and let us in.

"Is that what I think it is?" Paul asked, looking next to the front door by a small shrub.

I looked down and with surprise saw the doll that had been missing for almost two years — and now here it was by the door.

"Creepy, it's missing its eyes!" Amanda added upon closer examination of the doll.

I looked closer and indeed the eyes had been either ripped or hacked out of the doll's head.

I looked at Amanda. "That is definitely disturbing!"

I wondered if there was some significance to the eyes being removed; the doll seemed to be in fairly good condition otherwise. Was something not supposed to be seen here, or did someone see something that may have cost them some sort of retribution? Although the message wasn't very subtle, the meaning wasn't clear.

Amanda would occasionally step out from the cover of the overhang above the front door and walk out to look at the house. After doing this several times, she looked up and said, "Hey, there's a light on now!" We joined her; the second-floor washroom light was blazing through the block window. Darrin entered the property and joined us; we filled him in on what Paul had seen and pointed out the light now burning in the bathroom. There wasn't much we could do until security arrived.

"I believe that was a nursery at one time. The block window that's there now was originally a door to the stone patio above the front door," I told them.

We discussed our surveillance set-up and experiment plan: we were going to place two cameras in the basement to cross-pan the experiment field and those would be set up when John Mullan arrived. Camera 3 would go on the main floor, facing east from the bottom of the stairs. Camera 4 would be set up on the second floor, outside the westerly room facing the stairs and east down the hall.

Darrin walked out from under the overhang and looked up at the bathroom window and speculated that the light was on a timer. If I were a betting man, I would have taken advantage of him at that moment, as I knew two things that he didn't: the first was that it was a bathroom, and timers are normally used in main rooms and halls, and the second was that over the last two years of being in this house, I had never seen a timer of any kind.

I just looked at him for a moment. "We'll see, just as soon as we get inside." Just as I had said that, the security patrol car pulled into the property, parking behind Darrin's car. I walked out to greet him.

I introduced myself and mentioned that the light on the second floor had just recently come on. He stopped and looked up at the window, retrieved his master keys, and opened the front door. We all went up to the second-floor bathroom and checked the room. Nothing was found. Darrin shook his head exclaiming, "No timer!" With that, he turned off the light.

We walked the security guard to the door and he wished us good luck on our investigation. We toured the house, arriving back on the second floor. Paul had laid some powder in the most easterly room on our last visit, in which we had captured a print of a slipper. He was very interested in seeing if anything else was there after our absence. To our dismay, the room was locked. I called our contact, who informed me that no one had been in the house since our last visit, and that none of the internal doors should ever be locked. This room had been the location of a great deal of activity and now it was cut off to us. Paul knocked on the door; nothing happened. He found a key on the floor in the adjacent room and tried it in the door handle lock. It wouldn't work; he dropped it on the floor in front of the door, giving up.

"COME BACK! PAUL, PAUL, DEATH!"
(EVP EXCERPT FROM SURVEILLANCE TAPE)

We finished the tour and went out to the van and brought in our equipment, setting the command post in the large room on the main floor, across from the front door. We went about setting up surveillance throughout the house according to our plan.

John Mullan, Mark, Paul, and I carried the equipment to the basement; John M. unloaded his mobile battery unit and brought it to the basement on a two-wheeled dolly. Paul and I carried down the rest of the equipment. John M. started setting up the apparatus as I placed the speakers; Paul went to work placing surveillance around the room. In a few minutes everything was set and ready to go. John M. wanted to test the equipment. I agreed hesitantly, as it wasn't part of the original plan. John fired up the equipment and immediately there was a major problem: the LED on the frequency generator failed. Without this display there was no possible way of finding the exact frequency. I had signed this piece of equipment out of our work lab yesterday and, as always, it had been fully tested before being released and everything had worked perfectly. John M. tested and retested it several times, but there was nothing he could do to get the display to work. It looked like the experiment would have to be scrapped. With few options, I decided that we would follow the plan and try to get the approximate frequency. The best I could do was to give it my best guess from memory. I played with it, listening intently to each frequency as I moved down the scale. I knew this was going to be impossible. I found a sound that seemed familiar and locked it into the machine, then switched it off. For what it was worth, it was ready to go.

I didn't believe for a moment this would work, but what else could I do? We went upstairs and assembled the team, waiting on a couple more latecomers.

"DANNY BOY, GET BACK!"
"YEAH."
(EVP EXCERPT FROM SURVEILLANCE TAPE)

Paul took the parabolic microphone and went to the locked door on the second floor. He knocked lightly and immediately heard a heavy sigh come from a male inside the room. He moved down the hall toward me.

Meanwhile, the second floor camera was recording EVP of a male yelling, "Get out!"

We had to go downstairs to see who else had arrived because it had sounded like someone had come to the front door, but no one was there. We returned to the second floor and checked the locked door again, as if somehow it would be open now. Paul said he had found a key, but it wouldn't work. He pointed to the floor in front of the door, but there was nothing there. "The key was right there!" Paul said, looking around the hallway.

We searched the hall but could not locate the key. I could see Paul was becoming frustrated. "Was anyone else up here?" he asked.

"No, no one."

"Where did you find it originally?" I asked him.

"In here." He headed toward the room directly next to the one that was locked. "Hey!" he called out. There, on the floor, was the key. It had been bent at a forty-five-degree angle. He picked it up and it was hot to the touch. He handed the key to me; we tried to straighten the key as best as we could and tried it again in the door, but it just wouldn't work.

The rest of the team had arrived and John Mullan called us to come downstairs.

I briefed the team at the front door and then headed directly to the attic, where we left two team members and proceeded to the second floor, where Darrin volunteered to stay. We dropped one more member off on the main floor and headed to the basement. The team assembled in a circle around the field I had set up in the great room. John Perrone took a seat in the corner and was going to attempt to make contact. Sheryl took a seat at the top of the four stairs, looking back toward the glass doors to the yard.

I turned the equipment on and the thumping of the equipment started from the speakers. John P. said he was in contact with a woman named Elizabeth from the 1840s. For some reason,

I rolled the dial on the generator slightly higher, without telling him. He looked up and said she was gone and he was getting a man who didn't want us here. It was now, according to John P., in the 1940s that this person had existed in life. The surveillance camera picked up a sliver of light that came from the ceiling and passed through John P. There didn't seem to be a source, but the light moved as he did. The communication stopped, in part due to the hum breaking John's concentration; he rose from his chair, unable to continue.

I decided to leave the equipment running in the basement and have everyone move to the second floor. The two cameras remained operating, with a cross-view of the basement, as we filed out. There was no one left in the basement when the audio portion of the surveillance picked up footsteps, then shuffling sounds crossing the room, and then a disembodied male voice commanding, "Get back, Danny."

As the team arrived on the main floor, we split up; several team members continued upstairs to investigate the higher levels and a few went outside to see if they could encounter the shadow people.

The hum of the equipment was ever-present as the cameras in the basement continued to record. Then a different, slower male voice was recorded: "Danny!" "Kerry!"

Through the steady beat of the equipment, an older woman's voice was heard calling out, "Tonya!"

We heard stomping on the floor, near the stairs, but no one was there.

The older male's voice came in loud and clear. "Get out of this house or I'll ..." The end of the threat trails off, lost in the steady rhythm of the equipment.

The infrared camera captured a white ball of light growing in the standing wave; it started to pulse to its own rhythm. The light was present for twenty-three minutes, until Paul and I came down to check the tape's status; as we entered, the light vanished.

After our equipment checks were completed we headed back upstairs and the light returned, pulsing.

I could faintly hear the *tick, tick, tick* of my experiment running from the main floor when I noticed something. The tone had changed; something was wrong. I had to go back down to the basement to see what had happened. I was astonished to find the equipment had been tampered with. It only took a few moments to reset the machine and as I turned to leave a male voice called to me, "Come back!" as I later discovered on the EVP.

MEANWHILE ON THE SECOND FLOOR ...

John M. was captured by the surveillance camera while coming out of the servant stairwell onto the second floor and then going into the washroom. As he entered, the spirits were captured on tape, talking.

EVP, male 1: "Henry, are you there?"

EVP, male 2: "Yeah."

EVP, male 1: "He's in there!"

John M. came out and headed back to the stairs; along the way he stopped and turned, looking back down the hall toward the camera, then, after a long pause, he left the floor.

John M. came down to the main floor and reported that when he was on the second floor he had heard laughter behind him in the hall, but there had been no one there with him.

John P. suggested that we all go to the second floor, so we all moved there and assembled in the most westerly room; audio and video surveillance were operating just outside the door to the room.

"I want to try something that I have never done before. I am going to go around the room and allow each person to ask a question and see if we can get an answer through the pendulum," John P. stated.

We went from person to person in a counter-clockwise direction, the tape recording every question. We had no idea at the time, but two questions were answered directly, as we later discovered on the tape.

The first was Sheryl asking, "Is it okay for us to be here?"

The EVP reply was a male voice. "Get out!"

The second was my question when I asked, "Is Danny here?"

The EVP reply was a male voice. "Danny!"

I stood closest to the door to the hall and we heard noises coming from downstairs. Everyone was present on the second floor. It sounded like things were being dragged and moved, then I froze as I heard a woman scream. It seemed like it was coming from far away. I poked my head back into the room and quickly did a head count of all the women on my team — they were all present. Paul stepped out of the room and looked at me. "Did you hear that?" he asked me.

"The scream? Yes," I said, looking over the banister to the ground floor.

Paul, Darrin and I went to investigate, as we started down the audio picked up a male voice screaming at us, "Get out!"

We continued down the stairs. The tape continued to record whispers and a male voice saying, "Open the door."

We searched the main floor and found nothing out of place, so we all returned to the second floor.

Paul walked down the hall to the locked door, hoping that somehow it would be unlocked; he tried it and heard a heavy sigh coming from the opposite side. Again on the surveillance tape a man yelled, "Get out!" and then there were further whispers.

John P. felt he was being blocked and was receiving nothing but interference, he suggested that it would be best to go back down to the main floor. Everyone followed him down the main stairway. When he reached the bottom stair he stopped, said, "Right here," and sat down on it.

Everyone assembled on the main floor at the bottom of the grand staircase. Surveillance continued to record on the second floor, directly above us.

As everyone found a place to sit down at the bottom of the stairs, John P. was attempting to communicate with the spirits in the house. We lined our chairs up along the wall and railing to the basement stairs. I heard something from down the hall and strained to identify what it was. It was music, but not something I would expect to hear at this location. It was "Who Are You" by the Who. I went to investigate. As I turned the corner of the darkened room, I saw there, in the back of the room near the window, was John M. sitting with the eerie glow of a mini personal TV cast across his face.

"What are you doing?" I asked.

"*CSI* is on!" he replied with a grin.

I raised my finger to my lips. "Shhhhh!"

John M. shut off the TV and brought his chair out, joining the rest of us.

As John P. attempted to make contact there was a great deal of activity upstairs.

The following are excerpts from the surveillance tape as it continued to record on the second floor:

EVP, male 1: "Henry!"

EVP, male 2: "Hey!"

EVP: "Keep quiet."

Pause ... "Get back."

Whispers

"Let me out of here!"

"Yeah!"

Long pause

EVP, male voice: "Anna Rita."

Then the main door slammed. Although the front door is recorded slamming, no one had left the group assembled at the bottom of the stairs, and no one heard the door close at the time.

EVP, male voice yells: "Get out!"

A calming voice: "Henry."

EVP: "Yeah."

EVP: "Get back."

Incredibly, John P. sensed them on the second floor. "They are right above us! Richard, can you go up and see what's going on?" he requested.

I started up the stairs, with Paul following behind. As I reached the second floor I could see there was nothing there.

John P. called up the stairs from the main floor, "Richard, come back down and leave Paul up there?"

An EVP of a male voice called out: "Yeah!"

I returned to my place with the group as John picked up on a young woman.

"She is 18 or 19," he told us.

EVP, male voice: "Anna Rita, come here."

Pause.

EVP: "Hey."

As I took my chair to the bottom of the stairs with the rest of the team, John P. was trying to focus on the young woman. "She worked here," he stated.

A whirlwind of icy air pushed past Paul on the stairs, then past the rest of us. I saw Ben put his hand out to see if he could determine the cause and direction. There didn't seem to be a source, just a direction. "What have you got?" I asked Ben, who was sitting next to me.

"Something is coming past us!" he said, astounded.

I looked up at Paul on the stairs and he nodded. "They just went down," he whispered down to me. Incredibly, the flow curved, following the contour of the hand railing and swirled down the basement stairs, instead of continuing on in a straight line. The icy wind vanished quickly.

I looked at Ben.

"The wind curved around the railing and went downstairs," he said, smiling.

I shook my head, wanting to go down after it, but decided to wait and again focused on what John P. was saying.

"She is still in service here. She died young, tragically!" John stated.

John mentioned the bent key from the second floor. "They don't want us in that room."

Darrin sat in the doorway to the meeting room, listening to John P. speak about the bent key, and then he jumped up abruptly and ran down the hall to the glass doors at the end of the hallway. Instinctively, I followed. He was excited, cupping his hands above his eyes against the glass and looking out into the night.

"What is it?" I asked him.

"I saw someone standing there, watching us!"

"Who?" I looked out, but didn't see anything.

"It was all black, just black, leaning against that tree."

He turned and started down the hall.

"Where are you going?"

"Outside," he called over his shoulder.

I followed him and Paul joined us as we pushed out into the night, leaving through the front door and walking around the side of the house before making our way to the tree.

"There isn't anything here, no one is out there," I told him.

"But I know what I saw. It was right here!"

"There are no footprints, just ours," I said, looking at the freshly fallen snow.

His face went pale as he looked at the snow and looked back at the house, "I know what I saw."

I looked back from the tree and could see the group clearly through the glass doors. That's what this place did to people — it made them question their sanity.

"GET OUT!"
(EVP EXCERPT FROM SURVEILLANCE TAPE)

It was not long after that we decided to conclude our evening and began packing up, starting with the equipment on the second floor. The last thing that the tape recorded was "Get out!" then we turned off the equipment.

Everyone seemed excited about the events of the evening as we packed the equipment into the van. Most of the team would have stayed longer if we'd had the time. Some quietly reflected on what they had experienced and tried to make some sense of it all.

John P. met up with Paul and me as we were packing up.

"So how did I do?" he asked.

"I think you did great, but we'll see what we get on tape. The sound of the machine was a bit hard to work with," I admitted.

"I was getting all kinds of things, but I just couldn't concentrate with the noise it was making; it wasn't like that the first time you tried it."

"I know, the LEDs wouldn't work. I just couldn't get the right frequency."

"I got a lot on Anna Rita, and this girl, Tonya."

"Tonya, we have that name on EVP," I said, looking at Paul.

"What did you pick up on this girl? We must have been outside with Darrin at that point," Paul explained.

"She is a young girl. She doesn't belong here, she visits here. She died tragically and so did Anna Rita."

It was now up to Paul to analyze all the audio and video recordings to see what, if anything, we might have captured.

Paul tagged so many EVPs from that night that he had to go back and start over because he was losing track of them all. The entire process took him several days.

It was just after this that Paul made a new discovery that chilled him to his very core. He was sitting very close to his system and had the volume turned up very loud, as he usually does so that he won't miss anything. He had just watched me leave the basement when a male voice called after me to "Come back!"

Then a powerful voice broke in and said, "Paul, Paul ... death."

He turned the volume down and rewound the tape and played it over and over again. Whatever or whomever this was, it calling him by name. Was this a threat? A prediction? He didn't know. He turned the equipment off and called me at work.

He continued the review of the tapes and found someone calling for Danny several more times. Later in the tape he observed a very quick shadow coming from the experiment field that moved across the stairs, heading toward the main floor.

It was during the question-and-answer period the team was conducting on the second floor that several of us heard a shrill female scream coming up from the basement. Paul and I immediately moved to the top of the stairs and looked down, expecting to see something. We left the rest of the group and went off to investigate. After an extensive search of the main floor we had found nothing. It was the next day that Paul had discovered, while analyzing the surveillance tapes, that the scream had been recorded faintly on the main-floor camera and louder on the basement camera.

I met with Paul the following week for the review of EVPs and visual artifacts captured from the house.

"I'm not sure what the experiment accomplished, but it would seem it drove the spirits crazy," he said, looking at me.

"I couldn't find the right frequency!" I said, disappointed.

"From the very start, practically through the entire night, we have a spirit on the second floor yelling over and over at us to get out."

"What I found fascinating was when the experiment started and John P. sensed a woman from the 1840s, he couldn't see me from where he was sitting, so he didn't know I had dialled up the frequency and then, as I did that, he said he was in communication with a male and it was now the 1940s! I don't know if he was just receiving information from different layers of time from the house, or if it was the equipment cueing the varying time layers."

"I don't know, but we captured several things on this Anna Rita, she is eighteen or nineteen years old, a servant, what do you think?"

"I don't know," I told him.

"The voice calling her was male. It was creepy when he called her — he was trying to do it almost in a sexy voice and I'm sure it was the same voice that we've identified as Henry."

"They both worked here, it's possible they had some sort of a relationship. Who knows what that relationship was?"

"It's too bad the system didn't work. Are you going to try it again?" Paul asked.

"At this point I don't know. Maybe in the future. The problem is every time we do this experiment I have to borrow the equipment, and we need to try to get everyone together and you know that isn't an easy task."

"So what do you want to do next?" Paul asked.

"I think I'll invite the team from Peterborough down to have a look. They've been itching to do some work. I think it will be good to get some fresh eyes on this."

12

JUST BECAUSE YOU CAN
DOESN'T MEAN YOU SHOULD

On the following Monday I brought the frequency generator back to the lab and met with Mr. Hickman. I told him that
the LED had failed and I hadn't been able to run the experiment
properly. His radio was playing softly in the background as we
spoke. He put the generator on his bench, plugged it in, and as
he threw the switch two things happened simultaneously that we
were both aware of: the LED blazed to life and his radio started to
play "Highway to Hell" by AC/DC.

He just looked at me. "Hmmm," was all he said.

I thanked him and headed off back to my office. Not one to
believe in coincidence, that little scenario left me a little unsettled.

I sat down in my office and started calculating the frequency
and speaker output for a larger wave target when my office radio
started playing "Hell's Bells" by AC/DC. It seemed to be a big
day for AC/DC, I thought to myself. It was at that moment that
I decided to suspend all experiments with this equipment. Some
would say that I was being silly or paranoid, but what constituted
a clear sign that what I was attempting was probably dangerous
was not only the songs, but also the fact that the LEDs failed only

at the house and the comment made by my team member about End of Days. I already knew that what I wanted to do worked — as I had seen the results first-hand in the first experiment— but what I didn't know was what the impact would be. I called my brother and told him that these particular experiments were over, at least for now.

13

SIXTH INVESTIGATION

"DANNY, BREAK THROUGH!"
(EVP EXCERPT FROM SURVEILLANCE TAPE)

With the team assembled in the front yard, I was pleased to see our colleagues from Peterborough had made it for this night's investigation.

I met with Anita, who had never been to the property before and had no background information on it. As she stepped out of her van, she was immediately drawn to the balcony above the front entrance. I asked her what she had sensed and she told me to hang on until she understood what she was seeing psychically.

I gave her a tour of the house and as we reached the second floor she made her way to the south side and looked out the window, toward the lake and Joshua Creek. "A young boy drowned in the creek." *Long pause.* "Ah, and this woman, Anna, was a nurse-maid in charge of caring for him. She was so traumatized that she hung herself off the balcony above the front door of this house."

We had had our suspicions about what had happened to the little boy whom we had been picking up on our surveillance as

The balcony above the front door at Fusion.

EVPs calling him Danny and often referring to him as Danny Boy. We also knew from our EVPs about the servant named Anna Rita, so I found it extremely interesting that Anita knew all of this within ten minutes of arriving.

We finished touring the house and set up our base in the kitchen on the main floor. Dee had sensed a female who had rushed up to her as we had entered, but the feeling was brief.

Anita's digital recorder started to play in her kit, so she took it out and tried turning it off. When it wouldn't turn off, she removed the batteries. The recorder continued playing for the next two minutes without a power source. She checked the manual for the device and found out that all files would be lost if the batteries were removed because there was no backup power source for the unit. Anita put the batteries back in and the system worked properly again, its files intact and playable. At that moment I recalled the incident when Justin, the cameraman for the film crew, pulled the power on his video camera and it continued to operate as well. It seemed so incredible that electronic devices could pull enough energy to power these systems out of thin air.

Paul and I set up surveillance in the attic and on the second floor, and then moved to the basement where we installed the infrared camera in the large, open area. Paul wanted to place a second camera in the basement so I hooked up a wireless system near the base of the stairs, looking east. I was surprised when I turned it on to see two figures on the monitor, as I knew that Paul and I were the only ones on the floor. It took me a moment to recognize the figures as Dee and Anita, who were standing on the second floor. What I couldn't understand is why I had them on the monitor. I checked the camera transmitter and receiver, which were both synchronized to the proper channel frequency. I checked all the wiring and found nothing wrong, I had used all of these cameras numerous times in the house and this had never happened before. Ben came down and joined us, suggesting that I unplug the equipment and move it to another outlet. I did this, and when I switched it back on, the image was of the basement. I couldn't understand how this had happened as I had checked the second-floor camera and both the camera and receiver were synchronized to a different frequency than those of the basement camera units. Ben felt that the signal could have been fed from the second-floor camera to the basement camera along the power circuit we had plugged into.

Paul continued setting up equipment as well as a bell on a wooden stand, which stood just under a metre tall, his hope being that the child would want to play with it.

Anita, Krystal, and Sheryl made their way to the second floor, ending up outside the locked room. Anita knocked twice on the door. They waited for a minute and then two knocks came back from inside.

There was an audible "Shhhhhh" that was also captured by the digital recorder. The three now knew from the sounds beyond the locked door that someone or something was there. Anita tried the door, but it was still locked. Whatever it was remained, for the moment, safe from our investigation, and frustration in the team began to grow from lack of access this room. The women moved on toward the attic.

Paul and I were making our scheduled rounds, checking all the surveillance equipment, when we found the basement wireless camera unit was turned off. The tape, we discovered, had stopped halfway through. We reset the equipment and I pushed the "record" button. This was the same camera we'd had trouble with earlier. Paul and I climbed the stairs to the second floor to check that camera again, and as we arrived at the top of the stairs, the surveillance equipment captured an EVP of a male yelling at us, "Get out!"

As I checked the camera we heard the toilet in the men's washroom flush. I looked to Paul and we rushed down the hall to investigate and found there was no one in the room. Paul and I stepped into a room and stood quietly, listening.

The rest of the group worked their way back to the main floor, stopping in the kitchen to download digital audio files onto their laptop computer.

Krystal and Anita came up the stairs and headed to the bathroom. There was a male calling for Henry captured on the audio surveillance. Paul went downstairs and I waited for the girls to come out of the washroom, and even though the floor sounded extremely quiet to me, the tape was recording a male shouting, "Get out!" over and over again. The girls came out of the bathroom and we talked for a moment and then we all went back downstairs. As we left the floor a male voice called out, "Danny, Henry, get back!" and was captured as an EVP.

The entire team went outside to conduct exterior groundwork; the sensitives on the team found it quiet and could not pick up on anything. I let Dee and Anita lead the way as we walked the grounds; they passed the coach house and stopped, facing the forest to the east.

"There is something there, energy," Dee said, looking into the dark. Several of us snapped off pictures of the area, but all the photos turned out black, and even the trees were not illuminated by the camera flashes. Dee, Krystal, and I moved closer to the tree line and again fired our cameras, but once again all of the photos were completely black. Confused and frustrated, we turned back and walked around the house to the front door.

As we re-entered the house, a male voice was recorded on the second floor, saying, "Henry, go downstairs."

I ran up the stairs, on my way to the bathroom and again a male called out, "Henry, get in."

Later

We decided to break up into teams of two, as this would allow a team to be on every floor of the house simultaneously. Each team took their respective floor and rotated up to each subsequent floor in fifteen-minute intervals. At the first rotation the team that started in the attic went directly to the basement.

Attic

As Jen and I sat quietly in the attic, we started to hear sounds towards the back stairwell, but no source was found.

Second Floor

Krystal and Anita roamed the second floor. Krystal asked, "How do you feel in here?"

Anita: "Like a movie star."

EVP of a male: "Get out!"

GHOSTS

Main Floor

Sheryl and Ben were on the main floor. There was no camera there, and they reported that all was quiet.

Basement

Paul and Dee investigated the basement. Camera 1 with sound failed.

Dee caught a quick movement, but was unsure what it was. She felt that someone was near her and standing directly behind her. She asked whoever was present to please ring the bell. They waited a moment and nothing happened. As their time ended they headed up to the main floor, where they ran into Ben and Sheryl standing at the top of the stairs. Ben asked if they had rung the bell.

"No, we asked if they would, but nothing happened," Dee informed him.

Ben and Sheryl looked at her and both said at the same time, "We heard it ring!"

Attic

Krys and Anita arrived in the attic and heard sounds near the back stairs.

Krystal asked, "Is there anyone here?"

Anita was overwhelmed by a feeling of danger, and they ran from the attic using the servant stairs. The door slammed shut behind them as they left; they looked back up the stairs, toward the door and saw shadows moving at the base of the door. Anita felt it was a large man in his forties.

Second Floor

Sheryl and Ben were on the second floor, and the camera recorded whispers. They moved to the locked room and although they didn't notice, the camera showed that the adjacent room became very bright. The hall remained unchanged, however.

Attic

Sheryl and Ben arrived in the attic. Sheryl asked aloud, "Is there a man here?"

EVP reply, female voice: "No."

"WHERE ARE YOU!"
(EVP EXCERPT FROM DIGITAL RECORDER, COURTESY OF DEE FREEDMAN)

Second Floor

Dee and Paul came up the stairs to the second floor and headed toward the locked room. The camera captured a large, white, misty ball of light passing them and heading toward the camera; it seemed to have a ten-to-twelve-centimetre tail and was about a metre above the floor. The camera angle showed that it was not on the wall, but was moving in open space. The light arrived at the open room opposite the stairs, right in front of the camera, and made a turn around the door frame before entering the room and settling behind the wall inside. As it did so, another larger light appeared farther in the room on the floor. Both Dee and Paul seemed completely unaware of the lights.

GHOSTS

Second Floor

Jen and I checked every room on the second floor, and as we stopped in front of the locked room an EVP was caught on tape: "Henry."

As we turned to leave, a second EVP was recorded: "Danny."

Attic

When Paul and Dee entered the attic they sensed someone was there.

Dee's cheek was lightly caressed; she stepped back and asked that her space be respected. Dee then asked for them to touch Paul, but to Paul's relief, nothing happened.

Dee: "Do you want help?"

EVP, male: "No."

Paul: "Do you want us to leave you alone?"

EVP, female: "Yeah."

Dee and Paul encountered an extremely cold spot that came out of nowhere and lasted for a few moments.

Our time was up and we all met in the kitchen to compare notes. We all seemed to have had the most experiences in the attic. As we discussed our findings we could hear what sounded like a man clearing his throat in the attic on a baby monitor that Dee had set up there earlier. We decided that we would all go up to the attic, as a group.

As we reached the second floor, Dee stopped in the bathroom and the team waited in the hallway, preparing to go into the attic. The surveillance later revealed a male voice yelling, "Danny break through!" as if in a panic.

Then the same male voice, saying, "Danny, go downstairs."

The voice moved farther away from the camera and the EVP became faint: "Come here, Danny!"

As we entered the attic the camera picked up an EVP: "Dan."

We settled in and everyone heard sounds coming from the back stairs. Paul walked over and pushed the door to the back stairs open and several of us saw a sliver of light start at the edge of the door and slide up to the top of the door frame, then a shadow moved just beyond the door. There were no lights in the stairway. There were noises in the stairway and Dee walked over to the door; someone was there. We moved into the stairway and the sounds retreated. We shone our lights on the stairs and we could see there was nothing there, but the sounds continued to move down away from us.

We all went back into the attic and sat down.

Dee sensed a woman spirit present who seemed distraught. The camera picked up an EVP, of a female voice saying, "Help me!"

Dee felt the woman had now left and a man had entered the room; she felt he was not very nice. The camera recorded tapping sounds and shuffling near the back stairs.

We took turns asking questions out loud, hoping that we would record responses on tape. The later examination of these tapes revealed nothing.

After spending about forty minutes in the attic, the team and I went back downstairs for a break and to catch up on our notes.

Anita left the kitchen and wandered the main floor, stopping at the top stair to the basement and asking, "Danny Boy, could you go please ring the bell for us?"

EVP, male voice: "No, Danny."

The rest of us joined her and a few of us called for Danny to ring the bell. The EVPs were of the same male voice, also calling for Danny.

Dee called down the stairs, "Henry, could you get Danny to ring the bell?"

EVP: "No, Danny, no." *Pause.* "Danny, come here ..." *Pause.* "... run!"

We heard nothing and were not aware of the EVPs at this time. After waiting a few minutes, everyone decided to go outside for some air. As we were heading to the front door, the camera recorded another EVP, the same male voice yelling from the second floor, "Get out of here!"

To everyone's relief, the grounds did not seem as oppressive tonight as they normally did, and we spent about twenty minutes walking the property. Nothing out of the ordinary was detected and Paul suggested that we go inside. We entered the front door and as we prepared to split up to investigate the house we heard a child giggling in the distance. We could not determine the location.

Krystal and Anita headed back up to the attic.

There was no one in the attic, but the camera was still recording sounds, a female called out, "Henry, come."

Krystal and Anita sensed a presence when they arrived in the attic. The sounds stopped.

Krystal: "Who are you?"

EVP reply, male voice: "Henry."

Krystal: "Do you like kids?"

EVP reply, female voice: "Yes."

As they left the attic, the space was now empty and the camera recorded bagpipe music, not a song, but as if someone was practicing.

It was just after 3:00 a.m. and even though we wished we had time to do more in the house, the team was tired and it was time to pack up and head home.

It was a few days later, when I was going over my research, that this spirit of the little girl Tonya came up again. Her spirit was an anomaly. We knew by our EVP recordings that she was in the main house, as were the other spirits, but what made her different was she seemed to be the only spirit that would venture out of the house. We had seen that the spirits there remained inside, seemingly afraid to venture outside, while the dark entities remained outside. The two never mixed, except for this little girl. She was last detected by security near the main gate during the film shoot.

Was she just roaming or was she going somewhere? John P. had said she didn't belong here and that she was just visiting. There were hints of a connection between this mansion and the old farm across the road, but how much of it was true? I felt that in order to finally answer that question we needed to turn part of our attention to that property just north of Fusion.

It took us several weeks of research and visiting local businesses to find the right person to talk to about the farm. Finally we met Lloyd, a local farmer and businessman who had possession of the property. After some negotiations, he granted us permission to enter the house and furnished us with some of the property's long history.

I was extremely pleased that he was allowing us to work on this property, and I was hopeful that there was a connection between it, Fusion, and this little girl named Tonya, but these were nothing more than my personal hopes, because I really had no idea what we might find there. What I did know was that it was going to become complicated, as we had to spread our resources out over two very large properties at the same time.

14

FARM — FIRST VISIT

After a brief discussion with Lloyd, permission was granted to enter the old farm. When Paul and I entered and explored the once proud home of the Robertson family, we noted that the building was in extremely good shape for a house that had been built in 1856 and boarded up for more than five years. The house was a large maze of thirteen rooms, the windows were covered, and since there was no electricity, we had only our flashlights to guide us. The paint around the door frames peeled and hung there in long, jagged slivers.

In the darkness, the doorways looked like vicious mouths guarding the rooms beyond. We worked through the house, looking to identify hazards ahead of our investigation, and finding evidence of the many trespassers who had broken into the house to use drugs, drink, and try to conjure up ghosts (burning candles in such a place is a dangerous practice). I saw signs that even the trespassers were afraid of being in this house, for whatever reason; I guessed I would soon find out why. We found a back stairway off the kitchen, leading to the second floor, which contained two rooms that were completely segregated from the second floor

Farmhouse that was once the home of the Robertson family.

Entrance to the farmhouse kitchen.

of the main part of the house; I felt these were bedrooms for the staff. As we searched the rooms, Paul found a small box that contained locks of hair of the dead. Each lock was carefully braided with tiny coloured glass beads. Some were rolled in paper or a calendar page, and one such lock was contained in a page from 1908. Paul hid the box for our return, with better lighting, so we could conduct a more effective search and examination of the contents.

After a thorough search of both the interior and exterior of the main house, we headed off to a local restaurant to plan our next investigation; we knew there would be several major challenges to overcome. The first big one was the absence of electricity, which meant we wouldn't be able to deploy our standard surveillance equipment. The second problem would be the safety of the team, knowing that the building had been frequented by trespassers; we would need to secure the house and control access for the duration of our stay.

The following Monday, Paul and I returned to find Lloyd examining some issues with access. We also wanted to set some tape recorders in the house and see if we would be able to capture any EVP activity, if in fact there was anything to record. After a brief discussion with Lloyd, where we established which of his staff would open the gate for us on Saturday night, we collected our equipment and walked to the front door of the house. The sky was black and threatening and we could see lightning in the distance.

Paul entered first; the house was extremely cold. I followed and we started checking the house to ensure no one was inside. After our sweep we were satisfied no one else was there. Paul set a tape recorder in the living room and one in the master bedroom. We then retreated to the front lawn and waited for the tapes to finish. The rain started so we moved to my van for shelter.

When we headed back in to change the tapes, we both stopped suddenly after entering through the front door, as we

123

heard someone stepping on the paint chips in the living room. Simultaneously, we directed our flashlight beams into the room, but nothing was there. Because the house had been sealed for so many years without heat, much of the paint had peeled off the walls and ceilings, littering the floors. Every time we moved it sounded like we were walking on potato chips and that was the noise we had just heard coming from the living room.

Entering the room, Paul changed the tape and I continued on into the kitchen. Paul followed and stopped near the mud room. "Hey, there's a door here, I didn't see it before!" Paul said, pulling it open and revealing a gaping, black void beyond. The door blended with the kitchen wall panel so well that we had missed it on our initial tour. We fired our flashlights into the void and discovered stairs leading to a basement. Paul cleared a path through the spiderwebs and cautiously proceeded down while I followed behind. "There is water down here," he called back to me.

Paint chips litter the floor.

Paul stood on the bottom step, examining the basement. "I don't think the house has any leaks. I think the boiler for the radiators must have burst," he added.

The basement was a number of large stone rooms, and we could see a one-metre-square hole in the back wall and a large room beyond, however, we couldn't find a door to this area, which would be directly under the living room.

We made our way back to the kitchen and then to the second floor to change the audio tape. Paul moved the recorder to one of the other bedrooms and started taping. As we arrived on the main floor we heard movement in the living room once more, and again we found nothing that might have caused the sounds.

We moved to the exterior of the house and toured the property. The farm fields and barns were still being used by Lloyd and his family. We passed several workers as we passed an old stone building, and watched as they headed back to work. The sky was clearing and it was turning out to be a warm day.

We finished our tour back at the house. As I walked up to the door the temperature dropped, I stood a foot away from the door and it felt like air-conditioning was being pumped at full blast out of the house, it made me pause. We collected our equipment and started to plan for Saturday night.

It was going to be a very interesting night as we planned to conduct two investigations at the same time, one here at the farm, the other at Fusion.

Two days later

Paul called me when he completed the analysis of our tape recordings.

"So, what did you think of the house? Did you sense anything?" he asked.

"The house is wonderful. It's funny, of all the places we've investigated, this is the first place that truly looks like a Hollywood haunted house. I didn't really have a sense of anything menacing, just those odd sounds of someone moving around that we couldn't explain. So you tell me, is it haunted? Did we get anything on tape?"

He paused for a moment. "You need to come over and hear what we got."

"So we got something?"

"Oh, it's haunted, all right, I've identified at least four different people, two male and two female. It's not like Fusion at all. Whoever these spirits are, they aren't shy. But you need to hear the tapes. I think we will need to be very careful in this house."

I was very intrigued; however, I was at work and would need to wait to hear the recordings another day.

The next day I met up with Paul to go over the tapes. The first thing we discussed was the strange vibrations coming up from the basement through the radiators. We knew the radiators were empty and the only thing we could think of was the possibility of the vibrations being caused by heavy industry in the area. The next thing we talked about was the recorded sound of running water in the bathroom on the second floor. The tape recorded the squeak of the tap turning on and water rushing out, then it turned off, and then on again; there was no running water in the house, so these sounds were very strange.

"MY BABY!"
(EVP EXCERPT FROM SURVEILLANCE TAPE)

He moved on to a recording of a male with a very deep voice, he was talking in the distance and his voice echoed through the house, but what he was saying could not be determined. There was movement on the floor — a shuffling sound — the sound of heavy walking, slowing and dragging feet on the floor.

"I don't know what he is saying, but I just have a feeling that we need to be careful with this one!" Paul stated.

He set up the next tape from the servant area above the kitchen, and as we played through the recording what I heard pulled at my heart. It was a loud cry and a woman grieving, calling out, "My baby!" followed by more sobbing. I immediately felt her sorrow and was sorry for her loss. What tragedy had befallen this woman's child?

The next EVP was from the second floor, featuring movement on the stairs and then a deep male voice saying, "Get out!" It was a very loud and hollow voice.

"That's the same one!" he said.

"Well, he doesn't sound very happy we are there. We'll be careful," I said.

He stopped the tape. "Just a feeling about this guy — I don't like him!" Paul said.

From below there was heavy walking and the crunch of paint chips, then a male called up from what seemed to be the bottom of the stairs, "Who's there?"

Paul set up the tape from the living room on the main floor. We had just come in and Paul asked me if we should pack it in for the day.

An EVP of a young male (spoken in a very calm, matter-of-fact tone): "Yeah, they are going."

Right after this EVP was a very disturbing recording of a young woman. She did something I had never heard a spirit do before, she went, "Wooooooooo!"

This turned my blood cold, as it told me she must have known she was dead and seemed intent in trying to scare us. If this was true then I had a few concerns about what she might do when I introduced my team to the site.

The final EVP was the deep, male voice yelling "Get out" one last time just as Paul retrieved the recorder and turned it off.

Paul was right. There were four different voices, two female and two male. As we had discovered at Fusion, there might be more as our investigation progressed. Time would tell.

15

SEVENTH INVESTIGATION

Paul and Steve arrived and set up at the farm. When Amanda and I arrived at Fusion, I opened the gate and drove up to the mansion. The sky was black and threatening. We waited for security and the rain came in heavy sheets, making it impossible to see out of the car window. The rest of the team arrived at Fusion; Dee, Anita, and Krystal would make up Team 1, while Paul, Steve, Sheryl, Anthony, Amanda, and I would make up Team 2. We all took advantage of a break in the downpour and stepped out of our cars to meet on the front stair of the house. I could see Paul and Steve standing near the farm across the road.

Security pulled into the driveway and made their way to the front of the house, navigating the many small rivers created from the earlier rain. They opened the door and toured the house with us, noting a small flood from one of the front windows, which pooled in the servant stairway and basement. We walked them to the front door and as they left we quickly went to work setting up surveillance on the second floor.

Paul and Steve were talking in front of the farmhouse while waiting for us to arrive. All of a sudden, Steve felt strange goosebumps rise on his neck and the left side of his face went numb. Right beside them, Steve and Paul both heard a woman whispering. They could feel her presence, but could not see her, nor could they understand what she was saying. She disappeared suddenly and Steve immediately felt better.

The team from Peterborough wanted to do work in the mansion and agreed to spend the majority of the evening there, while the rest of the team would work mainly at the farm. We left Dee, Anita, and Krystal and headed over to meet Paul and Steve at the farm.

We pulled into the driveway and parked near the house. Steve rushed over to meet us as we got out of the car. He was very excited to tell us about what he and Paul had just experienced.

The team entered the front door with Paul leading the way. We toured the house room by room. Steve and I snapped pictures as we entered each area, and Amanda carried a small tape recorder. We had covered the main floor and worked our way up to the second floor, when Paul led us left to the blue room at the end of the hall. The entire team began complaining of feeling sick, dizzy, and disoriented, I felt a heaviness settle over me and what felt like a band tightening around my head. As we arrived at the blue room we looked in and Sheryl turned away, moving back towards the stairs. "I can't go in there!" she said. We quickly finished up our tour, Paul set a tape recorder, and we all left the house to get some air out on the front lawn. As we left the second floor the strange feelings faded away.

The sun was just about gone when Paul and I re-entered the house. It was like stepping into a void; it was so black you couldn't see your hand in front of your face. I had brought a box of small LED touch lights, which I thought we could use to at least give us some light around the more hazardous areas of the house. I put several on the stairs, two in the living room, and one near the servant stairs. Once they were set we went back outside to wait with the rest of the team.

We waited until the tape recordings were completed and again we entered the house. Paul and Steve went to the servant area to change the tape. Paul was replacing the tape when Steve heard a thud above him, as if someone had stepped off something and onto the floor. From his position at the top of the stairs Paul heard that it had come from the first bedroom. Steve looked up at him and Paul peeked around the door frame into the room, but he saw nothing. He hit "record" and headed down the stairs to the kitchen. Amanda, Sheryl, Anthony, and I joined them and we all heard someone walking above us. I looked at Paul. "I was just there — no one is up there!" he stated. The sounds lasted a few seconds more. As we started to leave the kitchen there were footfalls coming from the living room. Paul entered first and a large, blue light crossed the wall, passing in front of the fireplace and vanishing as it neared us. There wasn't a source for this light, and as it disappeared, the walking sounds stopped as well.

After a brief pause we made our way upstairs, going back to the blue room. Anthony and I entered the room and Sheryl tried to join us, but immediately felt sick — as if someone or something was pushing her away from the room. Steve started having trouble breathing. Paul stepped into the doorway and turned on the parabolic microphone, pointing it into the room. Paul looked at me with wide eyes. "Something is moving ... right next to you!" he said, looking at me. Everyone stood still and we could hear it move, the sound coming from over my left shoulder. It moved toward Anthony, and we could feel the static in the air. I heard its direction and looked at Paul, who was tracking whatever it was with the parabolic. Then, in a rush, a cold wind came out of nowhere and pushed past Paul and Steve into the hallway and in a moment there were heavy footfalls heading down the stairs. Whatever was there was now gone. I looked at Steve. "That room is the only room that causes my asthma to act up," he told me. We toured the upper floor, moving from room to room.

The front bedroom was a bit odd as all the paint had peeled off the walls and ceiling, but the floor was somehow free of debris. Paul set up the tape recorder on the stairs and was waiting to press "record." I directed the team that we should go outside and take a break. As we started for the stairs there came a loud bang from behind us. Startled, everyone turned, shining their flashlights back down the hall. We inched our way back to where the sound had come from.

Amanda pointed to something in the bedroom doorway with the beam of her flashlight. "What's that?" she asked. An old, torn plastic bag was sitting on the floor in the centre of the doorway; it had not been there moments ago. We entered the room and found nothing else out of the ordinary; there seemed to be no way for this bag to have moved by itself to the doorway. We made our way out of the house and Paul activated the tape recorder before joining us on the front lawn. As we stood there we could see the mansion across the road, completely black and dotted by numerous brilliant camera flashes in quick succession. I wondered what was going on over there.

We decided that we would get some food and coffee and break for lunch. Paul, Steve, and I stayed at the farm as the rest of the team headed over to Fusion to eat in the kitchen there.

As we ate by the car, Steve jumped, startled, grabbed for his camera, and started firing shots towards the side of the house.

"What is it?" I asked.

"I saw a dark shadow move by that tree and it went towards the back of the house. I think it was watching us!"

We investigated the area, finding nothing, and after a few minutes we returned to the car to finish our coffee.

"WOOOOOOOO!"
(EVP EXCERPT FROM SURVEILLANCE TAPE)

When the rest of the team returned, Sheryl had loaded a new tape and relocated the surveillance camera at Fusion to the second floor at the top of the stairs, facing east down the hall.

Paul wanted to let the tapes finish inside the farmhouse and suggested that we tour the grounds. Steve, Sheryl, and Anthony led the way with Paul, Amanda, and I following behind. Anthony was hesitant as we neared the rear of the house, and he commented that he didn't like it back there. We all had an overwhelming sense of being watched as we walked toward the barn. As we made our way to the end of the property the feelings intensified. Sheryl heard someone following them, just off the path to their left, and stopped to listen. She told Steve and Anthony what she had heard. Paul, Amanda, and I had stopped to look at an old stone building. They started walking slowly, intent on listening. They heard the footfalls again, just behind them, then movement near a bush, followed by the snap of a branch. Steve started shooting pictures, directing his camera toward the sounds. We caught up to them on the path and Steve told us what had happened, showing me a photo he took of the bush and with two large, bright lights glowing there. I examined the photo. There were no lights back there, nothing reflective, and the road did not pass behind this area, so it wasn't car headlights. I couldn't explain what he had captured. We all stayed together and worked our way back to the front of the house. The exterior of the property was becoming far more active than the inside of the house, at least in the sense of what we were feeling. The tapes were done now, so I entered first, followed by Amanda, Paul, and Sheryl. As Anthony was entering, Steve heard a rustling in the grass near the house, just a few metres away. He turned to look and heard a woman call out, "Come here!" Steve jumped up on the step and pushed Anthony into the house, quickly following him inside.

They all moved into the living room as Steve and I stood in the door way with the entrance and stairs behind us. "I just heard a woman's voice call me out front!" Steve was telling me when we both heard a sound followed by a rush of cold wind from behind us; a quick shadow moved across the wall beside us and we all heard something run up the stairs to the second floor.

I looked at Steve and he just nodded knowingly. We felt that whatever had been outside, following us, had just entered the house.

I felt a little uneasy. Was this the same spirit that had pushed its way out of the blue room and stormed down the stairs earlier? If it was, then we now knew it was a female and she was now upstairs somewhere.

"They are the hunters and we are their prey!" Steve said. I could see he was on edge. I instantly thought of that female spirit Paul had captured on EVP trying to scare us, and I was becoming worried that this was turning out to be a game for her. How far would she go? What might it cost us if she became carried away?

Anthony turned on the parabolic microphone and scanned the area, while everyone stood quietly. He listened intently. "I hear a man talking, but I can't understand what he is saying!"

He tried to determine where it was coming from, but was unsuccessful, as the talking stopped. He scanned for a few more minutes then shut the device off.

We collected our equipment and went outside to pack up the vehicles. I went to Fusion and met up with Dee, Krystal, and Anita, where we collected our equipment from there and went through the house, turning off all the lights and locking up. The investigation seemed to have been successful, at least in the sense of the activity that we had encountered; many strange, unexplainable events had occurred, which had been witnessed by all present. The evening left a few of us unnerved.

Dee, Krystal, and Anita stopped at the farm prior to leaving and wanted to have a walk-through of the property. At the back of the house Dee and Anita stopped at the same tree that several team members had commented on, saying it had made them feel uncomfortable. Anita looked up at it, "A man was hung there!" she said. Dee agreed.

"Like a suicide?" I asked.

"No, hung, like lynched!" she said nonchalantly as she walked away.

"Oh," was all I could say.

I wanted them to tour the house so I led the team inside. As we were standing at the bottom of the main stairs, discussing the house, Dee and Sheryl turned the corner into the front room and looked down toward the kitchen. It took a moment to register that what they were looking at was someone standing in the doorway to the kitchen, and then whatever it was moved off to its left and vanished. They called to us and the entire team moved to the kitchen, only to find it empty.

We finished the tour and the teams started to leave. Paul looked at the pile of tapes and told me he was going to need four or five days, maybe more, to get through all of them.

Mid-week

Paul called and we set up a time to go over what he had discovered.

The first thing we talked about was the reduced amount of EVP in the house. I felt that this was probably due to the activity on the grounds, I had a very strong feeling that the spirits in the house were coming outside and following us around the property and therefore could not be inside to be captured by our recording systems. This was going to pose a particularly difficult problem to overcome. We needed them to remain inside so we could capture any activity or conversation that they might produce. We had to find a way to reduce their interest in us, or perhaps we needed to leave the property after the tapes were set.

135

There were a great deal of sounds throughout the house, such as walking, whispering, and banging. There was one recording that sounded like someone was swiping objects off a shelf or table; heavy items and the sound of glass crashing to the floor in the living room. Paul played the EVP of bells, they sounded like Christmas bells, and kept popping up on the tape from time to time. The significance was lost on me.

Paul found very little from the recordings made in the servant quarters; the system captured some bangs on the tape recorder, a female started to talk and was interrupted by a great crash of glass, and after a long period of silence came the quiet cries of a woman.

There was an EVP of a female calling out, "Who's there?"

Paul loaded another recording and looked at me, "You have to hear this one." He set it up and I moved in close to the speakers. The voice of a young girl came on, clearly calling, "Mom!" Not only was this the voice of a fifth spirit in the house, but it was that of a little girl. We could only hope she would talk more on our next visit. We hadn't received any names yet, but acquiring this information normally took time.

FUSION SURVEILLANCE VIDEO ANALYSIS

Paul cued up the Fusion surveillance. "This one is great, listen," he said, as he switched it on.

EVP of a male's voice near the camera: "They're back!"

I had to smile because they seemed to be able to recognize us.

The same male yelled, "Get out!" and then banged into the camera; the image went fuzzy for a moment. There was heavy walking in the room with the camera, and then all went quiet.

A male called for Danny. A little boy started to cry and a young female called for Danny.

"This is really strange — this is when Sheryl relocated the camera in the hall," Paul said. The image came up: the camera was situated at the top of the stairs and looked east. There was a light near the top of the main stairway landing. Knowing the layout, I realized there were no windows near this location that could have caused a direct light or reflection on this wall, and it was apparent that there were no lights on, because there was a slight light in the foreground, which we could identify as the glow from the CCTV monitor, but there was no explanation for this other light.

"It gets better, just watch," Paul told me.

The door opened at the end of the hall and Dee, Krystal, and Anita emerged from the servant stairway and headed toward the camera. As they did so, the light on the landing left, it appeared, to go down the stairs. As they reached the landing a male yelled, "Get out!" and another male EVP shouted, "Henry!"

EVP reply: "What?"

EVP reply: "Go downstairs."

The camera was bumped and then failed.

I was truly amazed, but my focus was now on the farm. I wanted to know who was haunting that house, I wanted names from the farm. We had all of their names from the mansion, and I felt there was a connection between the two places. Paul just looked at me for a moment. "It took us time to get names at Fusion," he said. "It's going to take a lot of work to get them to talk at the farm. They may never give up their names."

"Then we need to work harder. We need to coax them," I said. We began planning for our next visit to the farm.

16

DAY TRIP — FARM

I had some free time, so I called Paul and asked if he wanted to go by to see if we could get some recording done at the farm. He said he would be ready in a half hour.

I was interested in seeing how the recording session would go, as we had noticed an odd difference in EVPs between us being there at night and during the day. The daytime sessions seemed to reveal more details, whereas the night recordings were limited. It seemed that at night, whatever was haunting this house was more interested in following us around the property, which didn't seem to be the case during the day. This meant they all remained indoors to carry on with their usual activities, whatever that may include. One thing I was sure of is that they would be talking to one another.

I picked him up and we drove out to the farm. We discussed our next investigation there and thought it would be best to try a two-night investigation, as we had found in the past that we could push activity up a notch if we didn't give the spirits time to recuperate. What I wanted to do was start Friday evening and proceed into the early-morning hours on Sunday. I was hoping this would push them to their limit and we might capture some extraordinary activity at the house. The only downside was that a violent outburst on their part was not that far out of the realm of possibility.

We arrived early so I suggested that we stop at the mansion because I wanted to get a few photos of the Fusion property before we headed over to the farm. We parked outside the gate and walked in. I started taking my photos as Paul wandered the grounds. I made my way around to the back terrace to photograph the view to the lake and Joshua Creek and as I came back around to the east side of the mansion, I saw Paul standing by the trees looking at the coach house. I startled him as I approached.

"Look!" he said, pointing to the main-floor windows. "Far right window on the ground floor."

I stepped in beside him and looked at where he had indicated, but couldn't see anything. "What?" I asked.

"At the window, inside."

There it was — someone standing at the window looking out— a mere shadow of a person. We moved in closer, never taking our eyes off it as I fired my camera at the spot several times. It moved and we stopped in our tracks as it turned left and vanished from sight.

Paul and I went to the front door and checked it, finding it locked. I moved to the window and looked in as Paul went around the back to check the other doors.

We met up at the north side of the house.

"It's all locked up," he told me.

"I couldn't see anyone in there from any of the windows I checked."

We waited for a few minutes and then walked back to our vehicles. "I think we caught him off guard." Paul said.

"Or maybe he was seeing what we were up to."

I checked my camera and found that the photos of the window held nothing more than sunlight and reflection due to the tinted lamination of the windows.

We drove across the street and arrived at the farm, parking next to the house. I called Lloyd to tell him we were there and he said he was working in the back field and would come and see us in a few minutes. Paul and I entered the house; we swept the house from top to bottom to make sure there wasn't anyone inside. Once we were satisfied that the place was secure, we began placing our recording systems throughout the house. The first we placed in the upstairs servant bedroom, the next was positioned in the second-floor bathroom. Paul pushed "record" and I pulled the bathroom door closed behind us. We went downstairs and placed the third machine in the living room. Paul and I both paused as we heard walking above our heads, just three steps, then nothing more. We waited a few moments, listening. We left the house and went outside to the van to wait out the hour it took for the tapes to run through. Lloyd arrived and we talked about what we had recorded in the house on our previous visit. Pleased with our progress and the stories of what we had captured on tape, he extended our access permission. We thanked him and he asked us to lock up when we left.

The time went slowly as we watched black storm clouds fill the horizon. Paul looked at his watch. "It's time," he announced.

We entered the house, I stood at the base of the stairs and Paul went to the first tape recorder. "Crap!" he said.

"What?"

"Someone shut off the machine!"

I walked into the living room. "Are you sure?"

He pushed "rewind" and then "play." The tape started with us walking away, then a few seconds later there were heavy footfalls approaching the tape recorder, followed by a click and then the tape stopped.

"Yeah, I'm sure!" he said.

"Let's check the other tape decks," I said, heading off toward the servant area. We pulled the door to the stairs open and Paul climbed to the top. "This one is okay." He ejected the tape and

141

flipped it over, pressing "record." We closed the door and walked through the house and up the stairs. Paul stopped abruptly and I almost walked into him. "What?" I asked.

"The door, it's open!" he said, pointing to it with his flashlight.

"I know I pulled that door closed." I leaned in and pushed the bathroom door open the rest of the way, peering in along the beam of my flashlight. Paul entered and checked the tape. "Looks good."

He flipped the tape and moved the machine to the blue room on the second floor and pushed "record." We headed downstairs and he placed the third tape deck in the kitchen and pushed "record." "Okay, let's get out of here!" he said.

We went out the front door and waited in the van.

When the hour was up we re-entered the house; as we stood at the bottom of the stairs a blast of cold air came out of nowhere and rushed past us, moving deep into the interior of the house. Slowly, we climbed the stairs to retrieve the machine in the blue room. I started to feel dizzy, but kept going. Paul went straight to the room and picked up the tape deck. We didn't speak, but I knew he wasn't feeling very comfortable up there either. We hurried back down to the main floor and went to the kitchen, where he picked up the second machine. I pulled the door open to the servant area and grabbed the third tape recorder. "Okay, let's go!"

The atmosphere in the house became oppressive, almost menacing. We were sure something was about to happen as we made it to the front door. We both breathed a sigh of relief as we stepped out onto the front lawn and into the sunshine.

Paul looked back at the house. "It's not like Fusion. Whatever is in there, I think it's more aggressive and we'd better be careful."

We locked up and headed home.

The next day Paul called and we met up to go over the tapes, Paul had found some interesting EVPs.

Analysis

Recordings from the servant area

Right after we leave this area there is walking on the stairs, the sound of someone jumping, either on the floor or a bed, and a child laughing and giggling, followed by three sharp knocks on the door to the servant area.

Second-floor bathroom, side A

The sound of fast-running water, the whispers of a man and a woman talking, conversation unknown. Then, clearly, the handle of the bathroom turning back and forth and the door creaking open. This was the same door that I had closed and later found open.

The blue room, side B

Heavy walking and the sound of heavy things like furniture being moved, then a woman starting to cry. Everything goes quiet for a few minutes.

The sound of what seems to be a rocking chair, three knocks, and a woman's voice saying, "Come up!"

Then a big bang, which seems to make the house tremble.

The kitchen

A loud ticking sound like a clock and walking sounds.

Another big bang rumbles throughout the house.

A male's voice: "Ah."

The sound of things being kicked or thrown around the room.

A young male's voice: "Jacob!"

I looked at Paul as we listened to the tape. "Who's Jacob?"

He shrugged. "Well, we're starting to get names. What about those bangs?"

"I have no idea, it sounds like a bomb's going off in there."

"This place freaks me out far more than Fusion ever did," he said.

"Even the grounds over there?"

"The grounds are scary, the house not so much; you know they are there and they just want to keep out of your way. This place, you have this feeling that they really want to hurt you."

"I was going to say, 'get you.'"

"Yeah."

"We'd better be ready for the next time we go in there, I don't want anybody getting hurt."

"We just need to be really careful, work in teams, and watch what we are doing."

"Let's make sure everyone stays back from that second-floor stair railing, I don't want anyone pushed over!" Paul exclaimed.

I made the calls and assembled two teams, one for the Friday night and one for the Saturday.

John Perrone called Paul out of the blue; he had not done any work at the farm and hadn't been advised that we had extended the investigation to include this property. John had been doing some remote viewing and wanted to ask Paul if we had moved on to the house across the road from Fusion. He had envisioned us there and wanted us to be careful as he sensed a spirit who seemed angry and enraged by us being there. He would cause us harm, but wasn't always on the property. He described the interior of the house room by room and tried to describe an unfinished structure next to the farmhouse, going on to say that it was a busy place and there were several spirits in residence and several more that came in visitation. Paul was amazed by what John had told him and he called me right away. We talked about the structure next to the house and remembered there was an open cistern there; we imagined this would look like a foundation for an unfinished structure.

It was interesting that John was sensing this dark force from the house and we very much agreed that caution had to be exercised by everyone visiting this property.

17

EXPERIMENT, DAY TRIP — FUSION

I had a nagging idea that ghosts created a slight static field that would normally be barely noticeable, but could increase, depending on their mental and emotional state. I've observed these fields during various investigations using my field equipment; they were there and I could measure them, but I wanted something more, I wanted to see their effect. I spent several months working out complicated methods of how I might do this until one day I was at work talking with an employee who working in shipping and receiving. As we were talking he opened a box that contained some laminated glass. When he pulled the glass from the box I observed something wonderful — small, peanut-shaped Styrofoam pieces that stuck to everything. I moved in and stuck my hand near the box and several instantly attached themselves to my hand arm and sweater, like little static balls. I asked if I might have the entire lot of them and the shipper was more than happy to get rid of them, so I gladly took them home.

I called Paul and told him I wanted to try something; a simple experiment at Fusion. When he asked which of the team I was going to bring along, I told him the experiment was going to be low-key and if he wouldn't mind if it would be just him and me. He agreed so I made arrangements to go out there on the following Saturday.

We arrived at Fusion, parking in front of the front door and got out. It was a beautiful day without a cloud in the sky. We had some time to kill as we waited for security, so we decided to walk around the property. We could clearly see the damage from an earlier windstorm with large tree branches and toppled trees all around. An ancient oak had fallen just to the west and its root system, which had run under the old pump house, had pulled the pump house off its foundation when it fell. A couple of window shutters had broken off of the coach house and were lying on the lawn. Fortunately, the main house didn't seem to have sustained any damage.

Security arrived; it was a gentleman who had let us in many times prior. We talked about the property and the investigation, and he wanted to tour the house with us, not something security often wanted to do. We wandered the mansion and I explained some of our finding as we entered different parts of the house. We arrived at the locked room and I asked if he might have a key. He checked, but unfortunately he did not. We walked him back to his car and said goodbye, then Paul and I brought the equipment inside. Paul placed a camera on the main floor and one on the second floor at the top of the stairs looking east. I checked the hall for drafts and air flow, subsequently sealing all sources with plastic and tape. To be sure, I rechecked the hall again and was confident that I had a good seal. I opened my bag of Styrofoam peanuts and spread them carefully out on the floor from wall to wall — not an easy task, as they kept sticking to me. Once I had a good base laid out, I switched on the camera and we left the floor heading downstairs to the basement to have a look around. The house seemed quiet, but I knew from past surveillance that the absence of hearing anything didn't mean they weren't screaming at us. We went outside to while away the time as the cameras were recording inside.

Two hours had passed and I felt it was time to collect our equipment and head home. Paul could review the tapes and let me know if anything was captured. As we arrived on the second floor, I immediately noticed the peanuts had been disturbed. The patch that I had laid down was scattered as if someone had moved through it and there was a path of Styrofoam leading east down the hall, and several peanuts stuck to the locked door and the door frame; this was exciting as it was obvious something had happened here.

We packed up our equipment and chased the Styrofoam around until all of it was collected and re-bagged. We then called security, told them we were leaving, and locked up the house. I was very excited to see the tape.

The tape was reviewed and something strange occurred; the video portion worked perfectly for the first twenty minutes and then became obscured by static, finally failing completely. The audio portion continued to work and captured quiet whispers near the top of the stairs and a man calling for Danny. Near the end of the tape a man yelled, "No, Danny."

"That never happened before," Paul said rewinding the tape and trying to adjust it.

"Normally, if a tape fails it fails completely, but we have audio," I said frustrated.

"Do you want to go back and try it again?"

"No, we don't have time, and I really don't want to become a burden on security, because they have a lot of work to do. Maybe we'll try it again another time."

The tape was disappointing, however, because the experiment showed that something had interacted with the Styrofoam and caused the patch to separate and move down the hall to the locked room more than two metres away. The only thing I could not tell without the visual from the tape, was if the Styrofoam was attracted or repelled by whatever moved amongst it? The tape of the first floor recorded an irregular ticking sound and nothing more.

The experiment seemed to have some merit; it was something I would like to try again in the future. Although I found it disappointing to a certain extent, I was accustomed to such things. You learn quickly that two of the most unreliable and unpredictable things on a ghost hunt are the equipment you are using and the spirit's co-operation.

18

EIGHTH INVESTIGATION

FRIDAY JULY 4
"TOO BRIGHT..." PAUSE "... TURN THEM OFF!"
(EVP EXCERPT FROM SURVEILLANCE TAPE)

Amanda and I arrived at the property; we drove up the long tree-lined dirt road toward the house. I found it remarkable that the house still remained in such good condition after being ignored for all these years. I parked next to the house and immediately called Paul on his cellphone to find out where he was. Paul let me know that he was only a few minutes away. Amanda got out and started to look around the side and front of the house as I began checking the equipment. Paul pulled in and parked.

We grabbed our flashlights and entered the house; it was cooler inside and we stood quietly for a few moments, listening. Everything was still and quiet. We searched the house and found everything as we had left it on our last visit. Lloyd had given us permission to turn on one breaker to power up the lights in the kitchen and living room; this also gave us an electrical outlet that would allow us to introduce an audio/video camera into our investigation. I was very excited about this, because as far as I knew no one had used this type of technology in this house. And since we had found at other locations where we had done this in the past, it gave us an advantage in helping to catch the spirits off guard and therefore capturing some interesting activity. I had great hopes this would work here.

We went out to my van to collect the equipment when Sheryl and Anthony arrived. We brought the equipment into the house; Paul wanted the camera positioned in the kitchen in such a way as to monitor the kitchen and part of the front room. Amanda and I started to wire the system up as Paul and Anthony ventured down to the basement to locate the breaker Lloyd had described. The basement was a cavernous area of stone and earth. Paul located the electrical box and threw the switch, and as the light above the sink in the kitchen came to life, Sheryl yelled down the stairs, "That's it."

Paul and Anthony emerged from the basement. "What a creepy place down there!" Anthony stated.

"The whole house is creepy," Sheryl replied.

"I'LL GET YOU!"
(EVP EXCERPT FROM SURVEILLANCE TAPE)

I turned the system on and we made slight adjustments until we found the right angle for the best view. Paul blocked out the kitchen window to ensure that there would not be any external light sources. As I switched the system to record, Paul placed a recording system on the basement stairs, and another one in the servant area.

As we all stood in the kitchen, Paul looked at me and said, "I smell bacon being cooked!"

"It's coming from here!" Sheryl said, moving closer to where the stove used to be. Everyone was sensing it now. The smells filled the entire kitchen as if breakfast was being cooked, and then, as if on the breeze, they faded away and were gone.

The five of us headed through the house and up the stairs to the second floor. Paul put a third recording system in the bathroom. I could see that Sheryl shied away from the blue room. "You still find it heavy in there?" I asked her.

"That room is so oppressive. I don't like going in there."

Amanda and Anthony stood in its doorway, looking in.

"Okay, everything is recording, why don't we go outside and look around the grounds and let the tapes do their thing," Paul said, heading for the stairs.

"We are leaving now!" I called out for the benefit of the recording system located in the bathroom and headed down the stairs behind the rest of the team.

The system recorded us leaving. A few minutes later there were heavy footfalls on the hardwood outside of the bathroom.

Caught on EVP, a raspy male voice called out and seemed angry, "Tell them ..." *pause* "... get out ..." *pause* "... this house!"

Then came knocking on the recording system, an irregular tapping, and the ringing of Christmas-like bells in the distance.

We went outside and toured the property; the mosquitoes were out in full force, the annoying little buggers kept us swatting and scratching, and sadly not a can of bug spray was to be found.

The house was now vacant; ten minutes into the tape there was loud banging and talking in the distance, the content of the conversation is unknown, then footfalls approached the recording system and a male voice said, "Jacob."

Outside we watched as the sun sank below the horizon.

"I feel like we're being watched!" Anthony stated.

Everyone agreed; the sensation was very intense.

Paul noticed something just east of the house, in the bushes near the barn; it looked like a small, isolated white mist or fog, which appeared in the opening of the trees. We all gathered in front of the house to look at it and try to make sense of what we were seeing. It seemed very odd, as the white mist, or what-ever it was, was very narrow, less than maybe one metre wide and a metre-and-a-half in height. There was no breeze, but the image swayed ever so slightly. Amanda and I decided to walk around and see if we could find out what it was. We headed off, leaving Paul, Anthony, and Sheryl where they were, watching it. As we arrived at the bushes we couldn't find anything, no mist or fog, nothing, but they were saying it was right there and we were practically standing right on top of it. But neither Amanda nor I saw anything out of the ordinary, and then, as Paul, Sheryl, and Anthony watched, the mist leaned in the direction of the old house and moved toward it, breaking apart and dissipating. We walked back and joined the others.

"Whatever it was seemed to have moved to the house," Paul stated.

"It was strange — I just felt like someone was watching me — it was overwhelming, and then to see whatever that was standing there, that was no coincidence!" Anthony said.

We all looked back to the spot. "Maybe we'll run into it again in the house," I added.

It was time to head back in and change the tapes; we entered single file, pausing to listen. Everything seemed quiet, or so we thought. We moved around the house, replacing the tapes. Paul decided to pull the recording system out of the basement. It had previously recorded some very bizarre sounds, such as running water, banging pipes, machinery operating, and a furnace that would come on and turn off, not very strange for a normal house, but one had to remember that this was a dead house and none of those things had worked for a very long time. It was as if this deserted house had its own memories of a life it once had and was now playing out those memories for us.

Paul and I headed up to the servant area, while Anthony stood in the hall between the kitchen and living room. Sheryl moved to the mud room at the back of the kitchen, followed by Amanda.

Sheryl stopped at the doorway, reeling back almost into Amanda. "There's something in the room!" she said pushing backwards towards the kitchen.

Anthony came over to have a look. "Nothing there!" he called out.

"But I know there was just someone there!" Sheryl told him.

Everyone seemed to be on edge from the sounds and visual phenomena we were encountering.

Paul and I joined the others in the kitchen and decided to wander the house and use our portable recorders to ask questions as we went.

"Everyone stay close," I advised.

We entered the living room and I asked, "Are you here?"

The EVP reply was a male voice saying, "Yes."

The tape captured sounds very close to me, like someone was dragging their feet, though none of the team members were moving at the time.

"Do you know a girl named Tonya?" I asked, straining, hoping to hear a reply.

EVP reply, female voice: "Yes."

The team moved to the living room. I was still using my hand-held tape recorder and the surveillance camera continued recording in the kitchen, facing the living room.

I began to ask questions aloud, hoping a response would be captured.

There were little bangs coming from the kitchen.

"Is there anyone in this house?"

No reply.

"Can you give us a sign?"

A louder bang came from the kitchen.

"How many are there in this house? There are five of us, how many are you?"

No reply.

"Is there a Tonya here?"

EVP reply, girl's voice: "Yes."

"Do you know of a Danny?"

EVP reply, girl's voice: "Danny!" There seemed to be excitement in the voice.

A very loud bang came from the kitchen, which startled us, and although we stopped asking questions, the tapes were still recording. We moved into the kitchen and as we stood there, scanning the room, an EVP of a deep male's voice was captured: "I'll get you!"

We moved across the hall to the front room, still asking questions; meanwhile, upstairs in the bathroom, the tape captured the long, slow creak of a door opening, then it slammed shut and bells could be heard in the distance. We were not aware of the sounds coming from the second floor.

After our question period the team climbed the stairs to the second floor, where Paul moved the recording system from the bathroom to the blue room.

We started to experience the nausea and dizziness again, and as Paul pushed "record" we were busy taking photos of the hallway. Paul joined us in the hall and the tape captured the sound of someone snapping their fingers twice, as if trying to get our attention and a male voice demanded that we "Get out!"

In the opposite end of the house, in the servant's quarters, there was the sound of high-heeled shoes walking across the wood floor, then something heavy was dropped to the floor and it rolled away.

The grieving woman started to sob and the sobbing became louder, almost hysterical, and she cried out, "My baby!" and the crying faded to silence.

It was becoming late and nothing seemed to be happening. We were a little disappointed, because other than the odd noise and Sheryl's encounter in the mud room, it appeared that the investigation was a bust. The tapes would later prove this wasn't the case at all; a lot was going on just beyond our perception. We packed up and headed home for a few hours of rest before we started again.

The Analysis — Friday

Even though we believed the house was fairly quiet on the Friday night visit, our surveillance told us differently.

The EVPs that were recorded were added into the investigation; the video analysis has been added here.

Video 1 with sound

A male calls out, "Daniel."

A semi-transparent image of a person comes from the pantry area and crosses the kitchen door, heading toward the living room. The lights in the living room dim by themselves.

A male calls out, "Cathy!"

The spectral image comes back into the kitchen and casts a white light on the wall next to the pantry, the light shapes are outlined in dark black, the odd shapes continue and spread to the floor of the kitchen.

A white mist comes from the pantry and crosses the wall and door frame, moving off into the living room.

As the mist vanishes around the corner the spectral image also disappears. Several snapping sounds are then recorded.

All is quiet until we re-enter the house, and the camera catches us looking around the corner, toward the kitchen from the entrance of the living room.

Video 2 with sound

The white light appears, outlined in black, on the kitchen wall between the pantry and the door leading to the hall.

EVP, older female voice: "Too bright..." *pause* "... turn them down!"

The lights in the living room start to adjust. First they dim, then brighten, then dim once more.

The light on the wall moves up along the door frame to the top of the door, then vanishes.

There is heavy banging all around the camera in the kitchen, and then all is quiet for a few minutes.

Angry male voice says "Get out!" followed by a loud bang, pounding down the stairs, the door to the servant area opens, followed by heavy footfalls and the sound of paint chips and broken glass crunching underfoot. The large, black shadow of a person is cast from behind the camera onto the kitchen wall. There is a heavy sigh and footfalls backing up the stairs to the servant area. The kitchen becomes very bright as the presence leaves.

Video 3 with sound

We exit the house and all is quiet. After a few minutes a whistle is heard — a child's toy whistle, the old plastic type with the ball in it. It starts in the distance and continues for some time, coming from different locations of the house.

The kitchen becomes very bright, cause unknown.

The lighting returns to normal and there are several bangs, seemingly from the living room.

A child sounds to be in a panic yelling, "Daddy, daddy!"

The door from the servant area opens and there is heavy stomping into the kitchen. The kitchen becomes very dark and there is movement around the camera.

We enter the house and as we stand at the bottom of the stairs, near the living room door, we are oblivious that someone is knocking on the door to the servant area.

We enter the kitchen and the lights in the living room become dimmer. Anthony and I walk back to the living room and Anthony turns them back up. "That was weird," he says.

I was awestruck by the recordings; there was so much to process. The question period with my handheld recorder and the EVPs I had received seemed to indicate that this girl, Tonya, did in fact belong to this house and seemed to know Danny, the little boy over at Fusion. Was it that she had gone there to visit and play with him? I was so impressed with the video images, but I was also worried about being in that house. It seemed that there were a multitude of spirits roaming there and we were walking amongst them. The video images were disturbing — at one point I am leaving the kitchen and the camera records this spirit moving across the wall directly behind me, mere centimetres from my shoulder. Some seemed to be upset, even angry, that we were there. My major concern was this male who made the threat that he would "get us." What did he mean to do? Would he actually cause us harm? Of course, I didn't know the answers to those questions; I didn't even know what was on these tapes until four days after we had ended our Saturday night investigation. Had I known, it may have caused me to pause before going back in there. But we didn't have this information yet, and I was preparing to head back in a few hours.

19

NINTH INVESTIGATION

SATURDAY, JULY 5

Amanda and I pulled up to the gate; it was locked. I called Lloyd, but he was on his way out for the evening; he had forgotten we were coming, and wouldn't be able to come back to open it. Paul parked next to my van. We unloaded the equipment and carried it by hand up the long dirt road to the house. The three of us entered and began setting up the recording systems. Paul went to the basement and turned on the breaker, while Amanda and I waited at the top of the stairs. Everything was set and recording so we went outside. Darrin arrived soon after and walked up to meet us at the front entrance to the house. It was his first time to the farm, so we gave him a tour of the property. He found the property to be impressive, but he couldn't wait to get into the house. It would later seem funny that in a few hours he wouldn't be able to get out of the house fast enough.

The four of us entered the house, touring each room on the main floor, moving up to the servant rooms above the kitchen. "This place looks like an actual haunted house," Darrin stated, as we made our way back to the main floor stairs. Paul led us up to the second floor. We all stopped and let Darrin continue on down the hall to the blue room. "What's up with this room?" he asked.

We walked to where he stood. "Why, what's wrong with it?" I inquired.

"It's heavy in there."

All of a sudden, like a wave washing over us, we all started to experience the all-too-familiar dizziness and disorientation, and it became very difficult to breathe.

Darrin walked down the hall and looked in the other rooms before coming back to the blue room, entering, and stopping in the centre of the room.

"I'm feeling anger, a lot of anger. I get this image that someone, a male, wants to slap me."

"That's strange. I'm getting a feeling of fear, a lot of fear, but these feelings aren't mine," Amanda said.

"Okay, let's go outside for a break," I suggested.

The four of us made our way out, skirting along the wall as we moved down the stairs, feeling as if something would toss us down if we weren't careful.

"That was pretty intense," Darrin stated.

We just looked back at the house, feeling better standing on the front lawn.

The remainder of the first part of the evening was uneventful; we kept changing the tapes and touring the house without incident.

It was after the sun had gone down that the house changed. We entered for another walk-through, inspecting the rooms on the second floor, then heading down to the main floor. Paul went first, followed by Amanda. Darrin and I were a few moments behind them as we had stopped to take a couple of photos. Darrin moved to the wall ahead of me, and, midway on the stairs, he stopped abruptly, causing me to almost walk into him. Then I felt what he must have encountered, an extremely cold, slow-moving force, like an icy pressure moving up the stairs, pushing us aside. In a moment it passed us and was gone.

He looked back at me. "What the …?"

I just shook my head. "I don't know."

Amanda stood there on the main floor, looking up at us. We were off the stairs in a flash and Paul rushed out of the living room. "I just saw a ball of light cross the living room — I think it was heading for the kitchen!" he said without taking a breath.

We all went to the kitchen; everyone felt like we were being watched. I told him what happened on the stairs and we decided to go outside to collect our thoughts.

The recording system in the servant area captured the sound of a rocking chair, its repetitive roll and squeak on the floor, and a woman crying softly. There was a long, silent pause, the silence shattered by yelling, but nothing intelligible was recorded.

As we turned to leave there was a noise from the servant area, then some yelling. Everyone stopped and looked to each other for the courage to stand our ground. We all moved together to the door leading up to the servant quarters. I pulled it open and shone my flashlight up the stairs. Paul and I inched our way up and cautiously checked the two rooms. We found nothing there, but that didn't mend our frayed nerves.

As we made our way to the front door, the lights in the living room flickered and dimmed, and we all noticed. Unbeknownst to us at the time, the same child's whistle was being recorded on several of our recording systems at the same time. It was coming from everywhere, sometimes in the distance, other times very close by; this went on for about ten minutes.

We retreated to the side of the house.

"It was so quiet last night," Paul stated, looking back toward the house.

"I guess they're all home now, did you hear that yelling?" I asked.

"It came from upstairs, I don't know!" Paul said, watching the house.

"The servant area," Amanda noted, shining her light toward the bushes.

As we stood there we heard banging, but we couldn't be sure of where it was coming from. Amanda took a few steps forward and stopped. "It's coming from the house!" she said quietly.

We all moved toward the house. The banging was coming from inside, from the walls on the first floor, from the windows on the second floor, from behind the many doors that used to lead to the wraparound porch, pounding, pounding. We all stepped back away from the house. I could see everyone was as frightened as I was, and for a brief moment I calculated the value of the recording systems and wondered if it be worth it to just turn tail, leave everything behind, and go home.

The pounding stopped after a few minutes, and the four of us crept up to the front door. I hopped up onto the stoop and stretched out my arm to fire my camera in through the broken front window. I depressed the button and the camera snapped a picture; just then, the large shadow of a person stepped out from the front room and crossed toward the stairs. I tried to shoot another photo, but my flash had not recovered. Startled, I fell back off the stoop into the weeds. Again we found ourselves backing away from the house. My heart was pounding rapidly.

"This whole thing is becoming out of control!" I said.

"Have you ever seen this much activity in one place?" Darrin asked me, staring at the doorway.

"Only twice before!" I told him. I didn't think he wanted to know anything more, because he didn't ask any more questions.

We waited a few minutes, then decided to go back inside. The systems were still recording.

EVP, girl says something unintelligible.

We moved to the front door and as I stepped inside, an EVP of a girl was recorded: "Oh, oh!"

All of us entered cautiously and stood at the bottom of the stairs. "He went that way," I said, pointing toward the kitchen.

EVP, male voice: "Tonya."

We toured the main floor, snapping photos as we moved from room to room. We could find nothing out of the ordinary; it was like we were playing a game of cat and mouse, and at that point I wasn't sure who the cat was, them or us.

"If it came this way the camera may have picked it up," Paul said.

On the second floor, the recording system detected us moving around downstairs. It also captured an EVP of a male voice saying, "Come quick!"

There was pacing in the upstairs hallway, walking slowly back and forth, then a raspy male voice, either trying to growl or clear his throat several times.

We stopped in the kitchen. "I want to check the tapes," I said.

Amanda and I checked the surveillance tapes and made sure everything was still operating properly while Paul and Darrin inspected the recording system in the servant area. As they pulled the door open to go up the stairs to where the machine was set up, there was an EVP recorded of a male voice saying, "Tonya, come here!"

Paul checked the machine and everything was okay. "There is plenty of tape left. We should go outside," he suggested.

EVP of a woman's voice: "Yeah."

They came down and met us in the kitchen and we started toward the front room. Paul said, "Jacob, this house is a mess!" and we continued walking.

EVP of male voice: "Get out!"

For some reason, instead of going outside, Paul turned the corner from the living room and started to climb the stairs to the second floor. Amanda, Darrin, and I followed him. I heard a noise, a creek on the floor behind me. I half turned and froze; standing at the bottom of the stairs was this solid black shadow

165

in human form. There were no features like eyes, mouth, or nose but somehow I knew it was a male. It was big, roughly two metres tall and the blob that would be its head tilted up, as if to look up at me standing there on the stairs. I forced my panic back; I knew there was no point giving into it because this thing stood between us and our only exit. Like static electricity, I felt tingly all over and somehow I knew it hated me, hated all of us. Real rage was in it and I knew it wanted to hurt us. How I knew this I wasn't sure, what I did know was my feet were now moving, heading up toward the others. I bumped into Darrin, knocking him backwards and stopping amongst the others at the top of the stairs.

"I just saw the shadow person at the bottom of the stairs. I think we need to go, it wants to hurt us, we need to go!" I told them, trying to slow myself down.

Paul peeked over the banister, looking down.

"I don't see it now," he reported.

We waited for a few moments. I wanted to go, but was afraid to move.

We slowly came back down to the main floor, and the fear that I had pushed back was now bubbling back up. I was now concerned with where it was hiding, if it was still watching us, and what it planned to do next.

We cautiously moved through the house collecting our equipment and finally reached the front door. As we reached the front lawn the banging started again, very loud pounding from inside the house. The sounds were so intense that I felt like the building would collapse, and then something happened that caused my heart to stop briefly. A woman's scream echoed from inside the house. The four us froze, and as the scream faded the banging stopped abruptly.

Amanda looked at me. "I don't know why, but I just got an image of a woman being dragged down the stairs."

I looked back toward the house briefly. "Let's go!"

We walked back to the road to where our vehicles were parked and started to pack up our equipment when a regional police car pulled up. The officer questioned us as to why we were here. I supplied my identification and letter of access and explained that we had just finished our investigation. The officer seemed intrigued and asked if we had seen anything. We told him about some of our experiences. He asked if he could come in with us and I declined, as I have a rule about people with firearms wandering around a darkened haunted house. He understood and looked up police calls to the property and showed there were numerous responses to the house for trespassers, vagrants, and squatters. He wished us happy hunting and left. As he did so we noticed that across the road all the lights in Fusion were blazing, when only minutes prior the house was completely black. I called Mississauga Security to advise them, and they immediately dispatched a patrol.

They arrived quickly and I met them at the gate. We checked the property and I noticed a door to the basement was open. We all moved back to the gate as they called the police to respond and investigate the interior of the house because we all believed someone had broken in. I couldn't wait any longer so I wished the security personnel well and left.

When working around old buildings it's not just the excitement of the prospect of ghosts that keeps you on your toes — anything at all can happen.

It was a week before Paul finished the analysis of the recorded tapes.

The Analysis — Saturday

Video 1 with sound

We've just left the house; there is the sound of footfalls across the kitchen to the side window, next to the camera. The curtain is moved and the fading light from outside comes into the kitchen. The curtain is closed and the light is gone, there is a heavy sigh, which sounds like it comes from a male.

A bright light comes from nowhere onto the kitchen floor; the child's whistle starts again and the light vanishes.

There is an enormous bang that echoes throughout the house and the camera shimmers, moving slightly.

Video 2 with sound

All is quiet for a long time, then there is movement in the kitchen, the crunching of paint and glass, and EVP of a male: "Cathy."

EVP of a male voice: "They are coming!"

All recording systems record the same thing, from the kitchen, living room, and servant area, to the second-floor blue room, there is heavy, loud banging throughout the house.

We enter the house and Paul and Amanda see two lights move across the kitchen. The video camera captures the lights as well.

It wasn't long after that we packed up our equipment and left the property.

After hearing and seeing the things in the house and my encounter with this shadow person, it took me a few weeks to decide to go back. It was not a decision I made lightly. Whoever or whatever this was seemed to mean business; it had no problem exposing itself to prove a point and this, coupled together with its uttered threat that it was going to get us, brought me very close to shutting the project down. But, as my brother reminded me, this is what we do and what we are looking for. Now that we have found one, we should do all the more to capture it on film. We started to plan our next investigation, however, I had to discount several team members for various reasons and for their own safety, and the others who could come, if they so desired, had to be made fully aware of the potential risks inherent at this location. After placing my calls, with one team member declining to come, we had our team assembled and were ready to go at the end of July.

This time we planned to use two surveillance cameras as well as the recording systems. I knew this would allow us even greater potential for gathering EVPs and images. The other thing I knew was that this dark spirit was already angry and we were about to make his house very small for him by using all this equipment; I had no idea what he might do, and that scared me a little.

20

TENTH INVESTIGATION

It was a bright, hot day. I pulled up at the gate, which was locked, parked next to Paul's car, and stepped out. Lloyd arrived a few minutes later, opened the gate for us, and wished us good hunting. We took our vehicles up to the house and found a shady place to wait for the rest of the team to arrive. Paul had invited John Perrone to attend the evening's investigation. I was interested in what he might see here tonight. This would be his first time at the farm and, as usual, we had kept him in the dark about what information we had already gathered by way of historical research and EVPs.

Before long, Sheryl and Anthony arrived and we went to work searching the house. We brought the equipment in and set up the surveillance camera in the kitchen, facing the hall and front room. We tried to find another working power outlet, but were unsuccessful and could not hook up a second camera. Paul placed recording systems in the servant area and on the second floor in the blue room; he also brought some bells, which he hung on a string in the kitchen doorway and on the door handle of the door to the servant area. As we were finishing, John showed up at the door. We all moved outside, deciding to allow time for the surveillance equipment to work and we took this opportunity to tour the property with John.

We started to walk the grounds and immediately John sensed two spirits who were brothers. He stopped next to the side of the house. "They are in conflict over the property. One has control, the other wants control. They want to do things in different ways. The one with the control fears that the other will get a say; he doesn't want him to have any say here and the possibility terrifies him for some reason."

He continued walking toward the back of the house, paused for a moment, and walked to the tree that a number of us had shown great interest in on previous visits. He put his hand on it and stood there in thought for a few moments. "This tree is depressed. There is something in its past. I see something swinging here, swinging from a branch, it's a young man — he can't breathe. I'm confused, because it isn't an accident, not a suicide, and it's clear he doesn't want to die." John pauses, stepping back from the tree and looking up. "I think someone hung him here — he was hung! Does that make any sense? Is there anything in the history about this?" he asked.

I remained silent and gestured that we should continue on with our tour.

John stopped and looked back at the tree. "That was very traumatic for the man."

He was quickly drawn to the cistern. "This is what I saw, is this a foundation?" John stated, referring to when he conducted a remote viewing session over the property.

"No, it's a cistern. They used it to bring up water from Lake Ontario and stored it here until they wanted to irrigate the fields," I told him.

John looked at Paul. "It's exactly as I described it!"

Paul smiled at him. "Exactly."

We walked past the barns and stone structures to the very back of the property, where we paused under a tree. "There's a grave here. It belongs to someone young," John stated, stepping back to look at the tree. "Again, this tree is depressed, just look at it, as if it were being pulled down. See how its branches are bent down towards the ground?"

"She died an unnatural death, and feels a lot of sadness over her passing. There is a woman, dressed all in white, who comes to this spot to visit the child. I would almost describe what she is wearing as a wedding dress, or something like it. I think if you ask around you might hear from people who have seen this woman, as she comes here often."

I had to wonder if this was what we had seen as the white mist between the trees, because this location lined up with where we had been standing. I was amazed that John had said there was a grave at the precise location where I had felt Tonya's body would have been buried.

Amanda noticed several large circles carved into the tree that faced the spot where we believed the grave was. They were interesting, as they could be some type of marker.

The tour wrapped up back at the front of the house.

"Well, you want to go in and see the house?" Paul asked.

"We just need to be careful," I added, as we moved to the front door.

We wandered each room briefly. John wasn't saying much and just seemed to be taking in information as we went. We arrived on the second floor and entered the blue room.

"There have been a few deaths in here, sadness ..." *long pause* "... This was a nursery at one time. The baby died at birth and the mother still comes here, cradling her baby and mourning the loss. She carries a pillow and rocks it, pretending it's her baby. I think it's the 1930s or very early 1940s. This is separate from the other part of the house, and there was another tragedy involving a child around the same time period," John explained.

I had read an obituary regarding the second family that had lived here who had a stillborn boy in 1937. Maybe that explained

173

why the room had been painted such a vivid blue.

John wanted to go back downstairs to what he felt was the heart of the house. We all moved to the kitchen.

Paul checked the surveillance camera, and Anthony and I took random photos as Sheryl listened intently to John as he analyzed his impressions of the farm.

"There is a lot of emotion," he said. "I am aware of lost love, things that didn't work, loss of a child, unfulfilled dreams, a great deal of mourning — an overwhelming sense of mourning in this house. The energy in this place lacks balance. Emotions that have been split, very depressed, and stuck. There is a very powerful and controlling spirit here.

"They can manifest change but choose not to. There are two main figures here, waiting for information. They are searching, looking, but blind to the opportunity to move on because they are stuck. Hmmm, blind by their own design; they're not really stuck, but are trapped by their own volition!" John explained. He stopped and looked at Sheryl. "I smell fuel, do you smell it?" he asked.

Anthony stepped in closer. "I smell it, it's kerosene."

John smiled, nodding. "Lamp oil."

As we were in the kitchen, the system above us in the servant's quarters was recording a woman saying something unknown, and the sound of walking on the floor and banging. There was a sound like a metal dresser drawer handle hitting against wood and a sound as if something had been tossed down the stairs.

"They don't know what to do! Indecisiveness. They seem to be waiting for satisfaction. They're very focused on the past: happiness, love, attachment, want — very obsessive. It's like when we are depressed, we just want to go back to our childhood when we had no cares and could just play all day!" said John. "Focused more on what he wants, missing the point, stubbornness, unfinished. He really loves this place."

He paused for a moment. "What can we do for you?" he asked out loud, then smiled, shaking his head. "Go away, get out, not welcome! They see me as a threat because I can see things they don't want us to see!"

"Let's take a break!" I suggested.

Everyone moved to the front entrance. Paul said that before we went out we should change the tape upstairs.

We climbed the main stairs, single file to the second floor. I paused at the top of the stairs and flashed my light down the hall to the open closet, and then in the other direction, toward the blue room. Paul was the last one in our procession and called out, "Who shut that door?"

The rest of us turned and looked down the hall to the closet, its door now closed.

"That door was just open!" I said.

"How could it close and not make a sound?" Sheryl said as we all inched our way down the hall.

We searched the closet and the two adjoining bedrooms, but found nothing out of the ordinary.

"We don't like closed doors, too many places to hide," Paul said, leaving the closet door open. Paul changed the tape in the blue room and we went downstairs and started to exit the house. Paul stopped and looked at Sheryl. "Hold on, I want to try something." Because during previous investigations in the house we had captured a child playing with a whistle, Paul had brought a whistle with him. He blew it twice; there came a bang from above them and then a sound as if someone had thrown a stone down the stairs at them. They joined us out on the front lawn. The recording system on the second floor captured Paul blowing the whistle twice, a loud bang, and then a different whistle blowing three times.

"This is a busy place, I sense a lot of spirits here," John said, looking at the house.

"Did you tell John about the dark spirit?" Paul asked me.

John looked at me questioningly.

"No, I haven't told John anything. I saw a dark three-dimensional shadow figure — it was very angry!" I stated.

"And he is going to get us! We got him saying that on tape," Paul added.

"He is one of the original owners. He's a big man, very angry, but no one is getting anyone here!" John said.

"We'll have to show you the box of dead people's hair," Paul told John.

"Maybe you'll get stuff from that," I suggested.

"Dead people's hair?" he asked.

"We found it in the servant area, they used to cut a lock of hair from a recently departed relative. We can see it later," Paul explained.

"Oh, hold on, I see. This hair doesn't belong to the original family, that's one of the reasons he is angry, he wants it out of here, he feels everything about it is wrong!" John told us.

Sheryl and I decided to go for some much-needed coffee and, as we left, Paul moved to a better position to watch the kitchen window, looking for any movement or shadows. John and Anthony joined him.

As they were watching the kitchen window, the audio portion of the surveillance system recorded activity in the kitchen.

EVP male: "They're out ... side."

Walking across the kitchen floor.

EVP male (panicked): "Get down!"

Then the bells Paul had placed on the door to the servant's quarters rang briefly; it was if someone had banged into them by accident.

There was a male yelling something in the distance.

Sheryl and I returned with the beverages and after a few minutes we again entered the house to change the tapes. As we entered an EVP was captured on the camera system in the kitchen coming from the living room area, a male saying, "Get back."

"If you're up to it, we can tour the house and see what you pick up on," I suggested to John.

"Okay," he agreed.

We changed the tapes and started our tour, beginning in the front room.

I switched on my handheld tape recorder as John found a seat.

For these sessions John used his pendulum, as well as his clairvoyant abilities, to gain insight into the history of this house and the spirits within. A pendulum is an ancient and simple device made up of either a formed shape of metal or a gemstone, which hangs plumb on a string. The premise is that the pendulum allows spirit energy to focus on it and allows limited communication by moving in specific directions. This process is greatly enhanced when used by a clairvoyant, as he or she can focus on the communication and gain a deeper meaning from the message.

"Is there a spirit here?" John asked.

EVP of a male captured on my handheld tape recorder: "Talking."

EVP of a female: "To me."

"Do you wish to communicate?"

Pendulum response: *Yes.*

"Did you live here?"

Pendulum response: *Yes.*

"Is it the 1870s?"

Pendulum response: *Yes.*

"1870?"

Pendulum response: *No.*

"1871?"

Pendulum response: *Yes.*

"Are you the owner?"

Pendulum response: *Yes.*

"Are we welcome here?"

Pendulum response: *No.*

John sensed we were seen as intruders. Communication stopped and the pendulum remained motionless.

"Would it be okay for us to visit the grave out by the tree?"

Pendulum response: *No.*

EVP male: "No!"

Once again, communication stopped and the pendulum remained motionless. "He's gone, I think that last question touched a nerve."

We moved to the back room of the main part of the house.

"What was this room?" John asked me, as we stepped inside.

"I don't know. It's an odd shape and there are French doors to the exterior."

Paul brought John his chair and we began.

"Is there a spirit here who wishes to communicate?"

Pendulum response: *Yes.*

"Do you live here?"

Pendulum response: *Yes.*

"Did you own this property?"

Pendulum response: *No.*

"Are you male?"

Pendulum response: *No.*

"Then you are female?"

Pendulum response: *Yes.*

EVP female voice: "*Yes.*"

"You love a good laugh?"

Pendulum response: *Yes.*

"Are we welcome here?"

Pendulum response: *Yes.*

"She is saying stay as long as we want," said John. "She is saying she has lots of sugar, 'my table is full of sugar.'"

"A cabinet?" Paul asked.

"She calls it her sugar table."

"I've seen old cabinets like that on TV," Paul stated.

"Sugar was a commodity back then, so it would be something to be kept locked up," John noted, then continued with the questioning. "Were you in service here?"

Pendulum response: *Yes.*

"She says 'I still am!'" John said, having picked up the information clairvoyantly. "Was it part of your duties to care for children?"

Pendulum response: *Yes.*

"Did any of the children pass away while in your care?"

Pendulum response: *Yes.*

"Were they buried on the property?"

Pendulum response: *Yes.*

"Can you indicate where the grave is?"

Pendulum response: *No.*

"She is saying, not supposed to," said John. "Do you know where the grave is?"

Pendulum response: *Yes.*

"Hold on, there is some confusion," John said, after a long pause. "I see, she didn't take care of the children. Caring for them was an emotion, not a responsibility. Does that make sense?"

Again, he continued with the questioning. "Do you know Tonya?"

Pendulum response: *Yes.*

"Tonya is familiar to you?"

Pendulum response: *Yes.*

"They called her Tonnie! Was her death natural?" He paused, sensing the response. "She says not right, her death was not right, she doesn't like to think on it. Does Tonnie play with the boy Danny?"

Pendulum response: *Yes.*

"Do they still play together?"

Pendulum response: *Yes.*

"She says they like to sing. Danny is very clumsy. Is Tonnie close by?"

Pendulum response: *Yes.*

All of us heard banging from the second floor.

"Is that the children now?"

Pendulum response: *Yes.*

"Do you wear glasses?"

179

John laughed. "She says glasses are for drinking."

Ask if she wears spectacles?" I said.

Pendulum response: *Yes.*

"She says, 'This is my room.'"

"It's a very nice room," John told her. "Ah, hold on, I see. This room was her room — a kitchen, the original kitchen. Could the back part of this house have been an add-on?"

"Maybe, we'll have to look into it," I told him.

"Did you live here a long time?"

Pendulum response: *Yes.*

There was a loud noise from the kitchen and we paused as Paul and Anthony went to investigate.

They returned a couple of minutes later, having found nothing.

"She says someone looks familiar," said John."By using the pendulum, can you point to who that is?"

It took a few moments for the pendulum to align toward Sheryl.

"Are you pointing to the woman?"

Pendulum response: *Yes.*

"She says you live up the road and wants to know why you are dressed like a man."

Sheryl was wearing jeans, a hoodie, and had her hair pulled back in a ponytail.

"I just got a chill!" Sheryl stated.

"Is your skin colour dark?"

Pendulum response: Yes.

"Did you come here from a long way away?"

Pendulum response: *Yes.*

"She says, 'This is my family now!'"

John looked at me. "Could this place have had anything to do with the Underground Railroad?" he asked.

"I don't know, I didn't hear anything about that," I said.

"It seems that she would have run the kitchen and that would be this room."

We went to the kitchen and examined the construction, finding many indications that part of the house had, in fact, been added later. The baseboards were different, the blocked-up door from the living room went into the pantry, which appeared to have been the stairs to the basement at one time, and the door to the kitchen looked bigger, as if it had been an exterior door at one time, as well as the large closet between that doorway and the living room. Even though the servants' quarters were located on the second floor, above the current kitchen, there was no access to the second floor of the main house. It was our conclusion that the kitchen and servant area was an add-on.

Paul noted two vents for a stove's pipes in what we now believed to be the original kitchen. One would have supplied heat throughout the house, the other would have vented to the exterior. This was further evidence that the kitchen was an add-on.

The audio portion from the surveillance camera picked up movement in the kitchen as we approached the front door.

EVP male voice: "Carol Ann."

EVP female voice: "Daniel."

I was surprised by the name Daniel, as this was another unknown name in a growing list we were collecting from this house. It was when I was researching birth, death, and marriage records that I came across a Carol, who in 1944 was a granddaughter in the family that owned the house. It is unknown if this was the same Carol mentioned on the EVP in the farm.

Paul looked at his watch. "I need to change the tape in the servant area."

We entered the kitchen and Paul and I went upstairs, while Anthony, Sheryl, and John waited in the kitchen.

EVP male voice in kitchen: "Hey."

Paul set up a new tape, and we came back down to the kitchen, closing the door to the servant rooms.

Immediately, there was an EVP on the new tape, a male voice

saying, "Get out." Then the sound of someone coming down the stairs toward the kitchen. The door did not open.

We left the kitchen, heading to the front door.

EVP from the kitchen, male voice: "Daniel."

The camera detected a wispy, white flash that came from the hallway between the kitchen and the living room, then quickly vanished.

As we left the house for a break, the recording system in the blue room detected footfalls in the hall, pacing back and forth, followed by several loud bangs. The walking stopped and there was knocking at the door to the blue room, and, after a moment's pause, the sound of someone walking away and down the stairs.

Outside, the night was quiet and warm. We stood around talking and watching the house and surroundings; it almost seemed too quiet. I had to wonder where this dark spirit was and what was he up to. The last time we were here he had been extremely bold and threatening, and now there was no sign of him. After the break, everyone felt better, energized and ready to go. We re-entered the house.

Paul, Sheryl, and I were standing near the living room. John and Anthony were near the front room when we heard what sounded like someone throwing a pebble into the living room. It hit the wall hard and bounced off the floor several times, and although we looked for whatever it may have been, we couldn't locate it.

We moved through the house and changed all the tapes and John suggested that we retrieve the box of hair so we could examine it. Paul and Anthony went up into the servant rooms and located the box, bringing it down to the kitchen so we could look at the contents under our lights.

John looked through the box, and, like a museum curator, carefully unfolded each paper he found inside for closer examination. Each paper revealed a lock of hair, some braided, some not. Paul noted that there wasn't very much grey hair there and thought most of these people must have died fairly young.

John read out the information handwritten on each paper. "Watson. Mother's, November, 1906. Austin, 1907. No name found, 1897. Aunt Aggie and Uncle Tom."

The original one we had looked at had no name and was dated 1908.

There were many unidentified locks, possibly two dozen more. I would need to focus on the only last name provided, which was Watson. I was hopeful that this would lead me to some answers.

The team proceeded up to the second floor and into what we believed was the master bedroom. This room was different from all the other rooms in the house. It was clean, although all the paint was missing from its walls and ceiling and the doors to the now-removed balcony had most of its windows smashed, yet somehow the floor was devoid of paint chips, glass, or any other debris. I turned on my tape recorder and John commenced his interrogation.

"Is there a spirit here who wishes to communicate with us?"

He perceived a "yes."

"Are you still taking care of this room?"

Yes.

"Do you miss the balcony?"

Yes.

"So you lived here?"

Yes.

"We found a collection of hair, would you know anything about that?"

Yes.

"Were they friends?"

No.

"Were they relatives?"

Yes.

"Is this the master bedroom?"

No.

"Did you sleep in this room alone?"

Yes.

"Did you pass out of your body and into spirit form in this room?"

Yes.

"When this happened was it the 1800s?"

No.

"1900s?"

Yes.

"Before 1940?"

Yes.

"In the 1930s?"

Yes.

"Are you a male, a man?"

Yes.

"Were you over twenty years of age?"

Yes.

"And you have chosen to stay here?"

Yes.

"Were you a Robertson?"

No reply.

"Were you a son of Mr. Robertson?"

Yes.

"I hear, 'like a son,'" said John, vocalizing his perceptions. "Were you related to the Robertsons by blood?"

Yes.

"A nephew?"

No.

"Like a son, he says, but I don't entirely believe what he is telling me," John commented. "So you chose to stay here because this is your home, and you love it here?"

Yes.

"And one day all this will be yours?"

Yes.

"So you are happy here?"

Yes (reluctant).

"Do you know what happened out by the tree at the back of the house?"

No reply.

"I don't know who this is, but I think he is trying to mislead us," said John. "Are there other spirits in this house?"

No reply.

"He's gone!" John said, ending the communication.

We started preparing to pack up for the night and the recording system in the servant area picked up an EVP of a male saying, "They are late."

Everyone said their goodbyes; we thanked John for coming out and secured the gate as we left the property.

Days later

I returned to the archives and searched for clues, finding that the Watson and Abbs family joined in union in the month of June 1941 because Ethel Abbs and William Watson were married. As for the other names, I came up empty on my search. As to who might have been the one to collect the hair as a family record, it was unclear.

We discussed the hair and the fact that, according to John, it was a Robertson family member who was upset about the existence of this collection, as they felt it wasn't right to have such things in the house. Although there were many different suggestions as to what to do with the hair, I felt it should be left where we had found it as I didn't want to tamper with the dynamics of the haunting.

Our time for working these two locations was coming to and end; we had now spent the better part of three years at Fusion and unfortunately only a few months at the farm, but our access was about to run out. I wanted to bring the investigation full circle and finish our work back at Fusion. I felt we had enough information on this person haunting the coach house and hopefully we could push him to communicate with us about what he did and what had happened to him just over seventy years ago.

21

THE FARM — DAY TRIP

I had some time available, so I called Paul and asked if he would like to go over and run a couple of tapes at the farm. He jumped at the idea so I called Lloyd and asked if it would be okay. He said yes, he was just about to leave for the day and would leave the gate open and asked if we could lock it when we were done.

Paul and I arrived at the farm. Lloyd had left the gate open as promised and we drove up to the house. The sky was threatening and we could see lightning in the distance, but it was dry for the time being. Paul retrieved his recording systems from the car as I checked the batteries in our flashlights. We entered the house and immediately we felt a pressure on us; it was different today. There was a heaviness that pushed down on us like we were underwater, and there was something else as well, a feeling of static in the air that tingled on my arms and at the back of my neck; a feeling that put me on edge. We checked the main floor and then moved up to the second floor. Going from room to room, everything seemed to be as we had left it from our last visit. Paul stopped to set up a recording system in the blue room. We then went downstairs and into the kitchen, heading for the servant stairway when a sound of something rolling across the floor from the front room made us stop mid-stride. We crept back to the doorway and looked into the room, but nothing was there. Paul continued on and placed his other system in the servant area and set it to record as I stood quietly listening to the house.

I led the way back out onto the front lawn. The sky was starting to clear and the fading sun peeked through the clouds from its position low on the horizon, casting long shadows across the property. We walked around the house and up to the barn, waiting for the recording time to lapse. On our way back to the house we paused, finding a good vantage point by the cistern from which to observe the area where the lady in white sometimes appeared between the trees.

"It's time," Paul reported as he looked at his watch.

We walked back to the house and entered.

"Let's get the one upstairs first," Paul said, starting up the stairway. I followed him up.

Paul stopped abruptly at the top of the stairs, looking from one end of the hall to the other. "What the …"

I moved up beside him on the landing and noticed that all the doors were closed.

"They were all open when we were up here before," he said.

"I know."

Neither one of us moved for a few moments as we listened. We started toward the blue room, opening and checking each room as we proceeded. Paul picked up the recording system and we continued down the hall to the other closed rooms. We moved slowly and cautiously, expecting to open a door and encounter someone at any moment. At the end of our search we had found nothing and no one to explain why all the doors had been closed; just an overwhelming feeling of being watched. The house had just moved significantly up the creepy scale.

We left the second floor heading to the servant area and picked up the recording system there.

A loud bang came from the front of the house. Paul thought it might have been in the living room, I thought it was near the stairs. My heart felt like it would stop as heavy footfalls descended the main stairs. Someone was coming down rapidly. We waited a second or two, then we rushed forward, cutting through the front room to the stairs, but nothing was there. We stood in the silence for a minute, both of us starting to feel anxious.

"Let's go," Paul said, and I followed as we made our way outside.

"Well. I have the distinct feeling we were not welcome today," I remarked as we put the equipment in the car.

"It felt like someone was up there watching us. I was sure when we were opening the doors we were going to run into something," Paul said, looking back toward the house.

"I think you are right, it was watching. Whatever came down the stairs afterwards sounded angry, because it was really pounding down those stairs."

We pulled out and Paul locked the gate behind us.

Paul called me the next day. "We got some interesting stuff on EVP," he said.

"That's great. I'll swing by and hear what we've got."

Paul set up the first tape from the blue room on the second floor. The sound of footfalls pacing in the hall were clearly heard, followed by six loud bangs.

"That must be the doors closing," I said.

The strange thing was that if it were the doors closing then they all closed almost in unison.

Then came a deep male voice saying, "Get out ... of here".

"That's it for this tape," Paul said.

I looked at Paul. "Well, I guess we were right. We're definitely not welcome there."

He nodded his head in the affirmative as he set up the recordings from the servant area.

"The first twenty-two minutes of this tape had nothing at all, then it starts."

EVP of a male voice: "Come".

Female sobbing quietly in the background.

EVP of a female voice: "Where's Tonya?"

"So?" Paul asked, looking at me while he shut off the system.

I was very excited about the recording. "This is wonderful. Again, there was our confirmation that she belongs here."

"I agree she comes from this house."

"We have a spirit who comes from here and goes over to the mansion. It shows they are social."

Sad news

It came all at once. I called Lloyd to set up our next visit and was informed that the house was now off limits for safety reasons and had been completely re-boarded and sealed. The good news was a new roof had been ordered and it would seem that the City was interested in saving the farm.

An hour later I spoke with Chris and he informed me that Fusion was officially closed because the mould situation was now out of control and the risk was too high for anyone to go back in there. I knew this day was coming, but still found myself unprepared for the news. The talk over the water cooler, as they say, was that the estate was to be demolished and a park would be left in its place.

It was difficult knowing this grand estate would be demolished. Financially, I completely understood, but historically, it bothered me deeply, as I knew these types of houses were more than just brick and wood, but contained the spirits of those who once dwelt there, along with all their hopes and dreams and memories.

I asked if we could conduct our final investigations on the property without entering the buildings. Access was granted.

22

DAY TRIP —
BOTH PROPERTIES

Darrin called and suggested that he and Michele would like to have a tour of both properties. I set up authorization and contacted Paul. The tour was set for Saturday and I wanted to keep the group small so it would be just the four of us.

It was around 2:00 p.m. when Paul and I arrived at the site parking at Fusion. I stepped from my car and looked at the new signs posted around the property warning of mould. I walked the grounds, watching the windows, looking for anything out of the ordinary; two cardinals caught my attention at the east side of the mansion, their bright colours struck a deep contrast against the grey background.

Darrin's van pulled up behind my car, so I walked back to greet them; it was nice to see Michele come out and apply her medium abilities to the project. She had only been out once prior and that visit was limited to the Fusion property only. Today I would have her tour both properties to see if she picked up on anything.

Michele walked over to the front of the house, looking up at the glass block window of the balcony above the main door. She quickly turned to look toward the coach house.

"What is it?" I asked.

"A man is calling 'hey, hey,' and it's coming from over there," she said, pointing to the coach house. "It's that creepy guy I encountered the last time I was here."

She ignored the taunting spirit at the coach house and again looked up at the balcony. "I see a window, but I am being shown a door. There is a woman, Spanish, distraught, a lot of tears. I see her fall, not reaching the ground. Pushed over, an argument." She paused for a moment, trying to understand what she was seeing.

"Oh, like a soap opera, affairs, rumors. But that window was a door. I don't know the layout inside the house, but the argument started in a far room, flowed into this room, and then out here to this balcony. She was pushed and ended up hanging there.

"Do you see who pushed her?" I asked.

"No, they are clouding my view."

We walked along the front of the building. "I don't feel the little girl is here. No, she isn't here right now."

Paul wanted to move on to the farm, so we piled into the car and drove over to the main gate, walking the rest of the way to the house.

"I hear a woman crying, sobbing, actually," Michele reported as we stopped in front of the house.

"Important people came here, stayed here, from overseas. I see a man in a uniform, high-ranking uniform from the First World War, from England. A woman is pushed down the stairs. Jacob did some bad things here."

It was interesting because we had received the name Jacob on EVP at the farm, but who he was or how he fit into the long history of this place was unknown.

Michele stepped back. "A black woman is distraught, crying and screaming. She is holding up her apron so she doesn't trip as she runs out the front door and off the veranda, then turning west around the house," Michele reported as she followed her impressions around to the back of the farm. "There are a lot of men, a real ruckus going on. Most are Afro-American and they are in a scuffle with a white man. There is the woman crying ... it's her daughter, the child is dead. The white male, foul-mouthed, he's a murderer."

Michele moved to a nearby tree and placed her hand on it; she immediately started choking, putting her hand to her throat, she stepped back and looked at the tree.

Michele at the hanging tree.

Again she put her hand on the tree and started to choke. Her head tilted to the left and she stepped back. "This man had something to do with the young girl. Oh, the bad man from over there," she pointed across to Fusion. "From the coach house. He killed the girl from here. The daughter of this servant woman. They caught him and he was beaten and dragged here, an evil man. He was hung here on this tree, not hanged like a broken neck, more like hung in the sense of being strangled to death with a rope."

We let Michele catch her breath and then continued east to the far end of the property behind the barn, where we stopped at another tree. The circle in the tree was evident and Michele put her hand on it. "Feel this spot. The tree is cold, but this spot is warm."

Each of us stepped forward and touched the tree and then the circle. I noted that it did feel warmer than the rest of tree.

"Someone is buried here; I get a name that starts with 'T,' a young girl. A lot of sadness over her passing," said Michele.

"Could the 'T' name be Tonya?" I asked.

"Yes, I believe it is."

Michele led us up the path to the old stone house. "John belongs here and so does Katherine. I believe this is a woman from the mansion across the street. She was seeing or had some type of relationship with John and was somehow connected to this house, but not the main house."

This was the first I had heard of something like this and had no idea how to verify the information. We walked on, heading back to the car.

"I get the sense that the spirits in the house want you to come back."

"Who, me?" I asked.

"Both of you," she said, pointing at Paul and I. "They want to play."

Michele furnished drawings of her perception of Tonya and Jacob.

I led the group back to Fusion, where we took some photos.

As we stood in front of the mansion, we heard a wooden door slam shut; the sound was loud and came from the west, where no building stood. None of us could explain it.

Darrin looked up at Fusion as we were preparing to leave and noticed the second-floor halls lights come on. We immediately reviewed his video footage of the house he had just shot and the lights were off. At least we knew there wasn't anyone living in the house.

Jacob.

Tonya.

Sketches courtesy of Michele Stableford.

195

The sun started dipping below the horizon so we all said goodbye and headed home.

On the drive home I reflected on the incredible way information is picked up by mediums and clairvoyants. Michele had never been to the farm and had only been to Fusion once, yet she picked up on the tragedies that John had talked about, and bits and pieces of information reported by Dee and Anita. It was as if a record of these events remained there, waiting for someone with the ability to tap into that energy. It seemed to be unwavering because it appeared that the information was the same for each person who picked up on it. The event as seen by them was always the same, however, some of the smaller details seemed to vary.

23

FINAL VISIT — FUSION

I arrived early, pushing the gate open and driving to the main house. I wanted to wander the property alone and have some time to reflect on what I knew about its past and the people who had lived, worked, and died here. It was a bright, sunny day, the birds were singing, the mosquitoes biting, and the squirrels were having fun tossing the protective rinds down at me from the chestnut trees. I didn't feel the oppressiveness, nor did I sense eyes watching me. The property was overgrown and unkempt. I noticed that the water level of Joshua Creek was very low, which was strange, as we had a year of record rainfall. My thoughts moved to Tonya and Danny and how they remained friends in the afterlife. I had to wonder if Tonya had been Danny's imaginary friend before his death and when and how they had forged this bond between them. I was pulled from my thoughts by the sound of an approaching car. I walked up to the front of the house and saw my brother Paul parking near my van.

"Is security coming?" he asked.

"No, we have to do our work outside tonight. The house is now off-limits because mould has been found in the basement and servant stairway," I explained.

"All those leaks," he said with a shrug, shaking his head.

I turned to look at the house and felt sadness over such a wonderful mansion being left to die of rot and decay. It was funny how everyone I told me how much they loved this place, and yet no one wanted it.

Sheryl and Anthony pulled up and joined us in front of the house.

"So, what's the plan?" Anthony asked.

For the first time since we had started investigating this property, I didn't have a plan.

"I called John Perrone. Maybe we can get some further information on this guy in the coach house," Paul said, fishing some equipment out of the trunk of his car.

John pulled in and we all walked over to greet him.

"I had a hard time driving here. I kept seeing a mirror between this property and the farm. The two places are connected in many different ways. There is a duality here, what happens at this place happens over there as well," he said, looking across the field towards the farm. "So, what are we going to do tonight?"

I want to find out more about three people, three particular spirits on this property," I explained.

"Which three?" he asked.

"Anna Rita, Danny, and the guy buried in the coach house."

He paused for a moment, turning to look at the balcony above the main doorway to the mansion. "Let's talk about her and the child first. She isn't resting easy and is definitely still here. She is full of guilt and grief; trapped of her own volition. She was a schemer, she had a lot of dreams, plans, all shattered. She was delusional because she secretly wanted to be the woman of the house. Danny was her son." He paused for a few moments. "Oh, she was an educated woman, an educator, a teacher, she could also do bookkeeping and she had her hand in everything. They trusted her completely, gave her a lot of power and control over a lot of things, she was treated like family and she used all of this to her advantage. Some of the help from the farm would work over here, not only in the early part of this house's history, but also, as the estate grew, they would fill the ranks of the staff here for extravagant events and parties. She would oversee some of this, and because she kept the books and paid for certain things she would find it easy to steal and manipulate the situation. They all trusted her, as she would take care of the kids and teach them not only here, but also at the farm. When things were moving between these two properties she would be in the middle; she found it easy. They would hand her a large sum of money and tell her, 'Set up for this party, sweetie,' and she would haggle and barter to under-cut the cost, keep what money was left and produce receipts for the full amount.

"She, for some reason, let Danny know what her plans were, and afterwards realized he would be a threat to her plans and position if he told anyone. She felt she had to do something before she was discovered and it was she who killed him. She thought it would be easy, but it wasn't, and she suffered for her actions. Danny had told someone this secret before his death and they had staged her murder to appear to be a suicide; it was perfect, as they used the cover story of her grief over the loss of Danny as her motive." John stopped and looked up at the balcony again. "She is there, I sense she was drugged and she has bruising on her face. I think she had an affair here at this house with someone very important, but she also had an affair with someone important over at the farm as well. I think when Danny was born no one really knew whose son he was and she quietly implied to each man that he was maybe theirs. She used Danny as a pawn, even though Danny was actually Hen-ry's son. It would have been like walking on eggshells around here, and that's why she was given so much freedom. Well, that house of cards came crashing down around her."

The sound of a door slamming came from the direction of the coach house.

"So, going back to the mirror image I saw between these two properties, the duality. Affair here and affair there, the guy hung over there in the tree, and she was hung off the balcony over here. Tonya was buried over there, and this guy was buried in the coach house here. Tonya died due to an act of violence over here, and her killer died by violence over there. It's very strange, what happens there happens here, even the loss of the kids. There seems to be a deeper connection between these two properties."

We stopped for a break. Paul and Anthony walked east, heading between the coach house and the mansion. John, Sheryl, and I stood talking in the circular driveway in front of the house. The sun had gone down and it was cooling off, with enough of a breeze to keep the mosquitoes away from us. Anthony came back first and joined us. Paul came back, excited, he reported seeing a solid black figure cross the meeting room at the far end of the house. He said he was looking through the glass doors at the east end of the house when this figure crossed the floor.

"That's what I saw one of the first times we were here," John said.

We all went over to the doors to have a look, but unfortunately whoever or whatever it was didn't make a return visit.

We went back to our post in the driveway.

"Okay, I want to know more about this guy in the coach house," I asserted.

"The guy in the coach house, he is not resting. He worked out in the sun, was very fond of children, and would always carry a stick of gum or a piece of candy on him. He had a way with words; he could present himself as almost an angel, but this guy was a killer. He had seen and spoken to the girl several times and had found it easy to manipulate her, he passed judgment on her. What he did to this girl was terrible, and what ended up happening to this guy was justifiable."

He paused for a moment. "Oh, she wasn't the first child he did this to. He had done this sort of thing before. I don't think he wanted me to see that because he's angry and has his back to us. I can tell you he has no regrets, except for being caught. He is saying, 'I work here, why are you bothering me about such things?'"

"Maybe he was framed," Paul suggested.

"No, he was caught red-handed, he can sure spin a tale. He is a psychopath."

John stopped for a moment. "That's all I'm getting, he is trying to block me from seeing anything else."

"Maybe it was the 'psycho' comment? So that's it, then," I said.

"There is something I would like to try. I don't know if it will work, because I've never done this before, but I want to see if he will tell us something specific through the tarot cards." John took his cards from a protective bag and leaned over the trunk of his car, shuffling them.

"Okay, let's see. This is your last opportunity to tell us whatever you have to say."

John started to flip the cards over, intuitively knowing what was coming next. He started channelling the words of the spirit.

Tarot reading at the coach house.

"Listen to me! Don't mess with me, I have power and resources, I'll tie you up and stab you in the heart, I'll put you in the grave! I will kill you!"

The cards came so fast we had to look at them again, and when John had finished, he explained each card to us. "Like I said, a psychopath!"

"And he sounds a little bit scared," I added.

We stood in the driveway and reminisced about all the things we had experienced over the last three years. I felt for these families; the tragedies that had befallen them, so much sadness and loss, the things that made spirits haunt places like this were such powerful memories acting like anchors and holding them here.

Well, we had come full circle. I had to wonder what other mysteries still remained hidden here. But as far as I was concerned, our investigations were over. I took a moment to quietly say goodbye to the grand old place and the spirits I had encountered here.

We all said our goodbyes and drove out of that place, a place called Fusion.

24

PARTING THOUGHTS

After careful analysis of the surveillance tapes, the audio portions in particular, we began to build a story of what was taking place between the spirit boy known as Danny and the older male spirit, identified as Henry. The relationship seemed to be that Henry was charged with the responsibility of keeping Danny safe. There also seemed to be a relationship between Henry and Anna Rita, but we could not fully determine what that relationship was. We do know, however, that they were both employed in the service of this grand estate. It could not be determined why the spirits at Fusion perceived us as a threat, however, it was obvious that they did see us as a major concern. Henry was constantly directing Danny to do things either to avoid us or to escape us. The other spirits didn't seem to deal directly with Danny, with the exception of Anna Rita from time to time, but rather Henry would be directed by other spirits to deal with Danny. They would notify Henry if Danny was becoming too close to us and therefore he needed to respond and order Danny to get back or get away. The best example of this was Henry telling Danny to break through as we stood between Henry and Danny on the second floor, and when that wasn't an option, Henry demanded that Danny go downstairs to avoid us. He constantly directed Danny to get back, and when a team member requested Danny to ring the bell, Henry barked out a stern warning, "No."

Could it be Anna Rita who continued to maintain the servant stairway and keep it dust-free and polished in a house where nothing had been cleaned in years? Does she remain there, feeling that she failed the boy when he died and somehow has to repay some sort of debt? Was it true that she was responsible for his death? Was it guilt that held her here?

The dark entities on the property gave rise to many questions in our investigation. Who or what were they? Why were they here? What, if anything, did they want? The government had mentioned that there were archaeological interests on the property; this meant there were Native burial grounds nearby. But something wasn't quite right about these entities as we had, on previous investigations, run into Native spirits and they acted and responded as any spirit would. They usually had a story or message to tell or wished to deliver a warning. But whatever these entities were, they were either unable or unwilling to communicate with us. The three sensitives I had brought to the property all reported similar findings; they could sense their presence or energies, but nothing further. There was what they described as a void around them, and where other spirits would make contact or at least block themselves from the medium, in itself a form of communication, in this specific case there was nothing. One of the mediums described it as, "The line is open but there is nothing there but static."

I had to wonder what exactly Hydro had done on this property and if they had something to do with these dark spirits. Did Hydro, for example, during the pursuit of cold-fusion technology, cause damage to the fabric of time/space at the site and inadvertently open a doorway to another reality, allowing these dark entities to become trapped here? Whatever they were, they seemed to have a deep interest in who we were and what we were doing on the property.

The buildings represented a typical haunting and, as in every case, there were associated anomalies, however, there was nothing typical about the things on the grounds. I had to take into account all the extreme occurrences that continually took place here, like the bizarre roving electromagnetic fields, the anomalous floating frequencies of two and four hertz that we had detected, not to mention the failure of cellphones and other electrical equipment. This also included strange time variations in synchronized timing systems and the failure of satellite-based information systems. How about the strange occurrences when equipment operated without a power source? It seemed that time and space may have been shattered here and things drifted in and out, acting and reacting to us, our equipment, and our environment. Could these dark entities be from another dimension? Possibly. Do we profess to have proof? No!

"KATHLEEN"
(EVP EXCERPT FROM SURVEILLANCE TAPE)

The woman that John P. first detected is believed to be Kathleen, the matriarch of the household who tried to hold together her home and family. There is no evidence that James is present, however. As there is an unknown male who has directed Henry to look after Danny Boy, the team feels that this person is most likely Charles, Kathleen's first husband. However, it would seem he is only there periodically, in visitation. Henry and Anna Rita appear to be servants who have a deep attachment to the house and to Kathleen, as well as a deep responsibility to the child, Danny. We feel that Danny was the child of this servant couple and was most likely the main force drawing them back to the house after their death. It was likely that the carriage hidden in the coach house crawl space was Danny's. We feel that Henry was in charge of the servants and was from time to time referred to as Captain.

Kathleen was torn between the loss of her first husband by death and her second husband James by divorce. She revelled in the grand times that took place in the house, and despaired of her second marriage of nineteen years ending in divorce; she would have been devastated as James ripped up his gallery and moved off to be with his new love, who would become his third wife. Left with few options, Kathleen sold the property to Hydro and moved to Toronto.

Upon her death in 1991, it would seem that her spirit returned to the mansion and to a time of greatness, of extravagant parties and wonderful social activities, but with the good came the bad and the memories of love lost.

Tonya was far more difficult to figure out, as we could find no records for her at Fusion where she was first detected; she inspired the team in being the only spirit confident enough to leave the house and move around outside on the grounds. It was her actions that led us to the farmhouse, and it was there that we made the startling discovery of who she was and how social she was, visiting Danny and the Bell estate, where she seems to have been readily accepted. She seemed to be the daughter of a woman who served the family who lived at the farm, and she herself resided in the servant's quarters.

The many spirits at the farm posed some difficulty, as the property was so old that many layers of time existed there. It was hard to place what spirit belonged to which time, but most seemed to be aware of the others who haunted the old homestead and interacted well with each other. Several, we discovered, were well aware that they were dead and perceived us easily as we came and went on this grand property. The woman who wandered the house and grounds doing almost stereotypical ghost stuff truly touched my heart; she genuinely had a great sense of humor and it seemed that she felt she had a duty to do what ghosts supposedly did. Nothing told me this more clearly than as when she gave us an EVP of herself going, "Woooooo!" in trying to be ghost-like.

The dark spirit was also fully aware that he was dead and had the ability to perceive us, and he did so, keeping watch over every move we made when on the property.

I feel he was more than likely one of the owners of the farm, although I do not know which one. He showed rage at us being there and quite possibly saw us as the same type of trespassers who had frequently used the house for all types of reasons, most of which would have been seen as immoral and harmful by him.

I spoke to the local police and they confirmed numerous visits to the property to deal with vagrants and squatters going back to 2003. Although he caused me great concern, I feel his intentions were, simply put, to protect his home and family from outsiders.

More bizarre was John's vision of the mirror; what it meant is anyone's guess, but the similarities and parallels between these two properties are astonishing, to say the least.

25

THEORY OF WHAT
MAY HAVE HAPPENED

Y ou have read the witness accounts and events that brought us
from that first strange introduction to Fusion to the final investigation at the farm. The spirits we encountered there are guarded
and continue in their own reality. Each has their own fascinating
story and each conducts their own personal daily business. But
there is a darker story, a tragic set of events that occurred, covered up so effectively that very little evidence remains today. The
story unfolds in the collection of EVPs recorded and in the testimony of three separate and independent mediums. Is what I am
about to write possible? Yes. Can we prove it? No. It is only a theory and will remain up to the reader to decide. Quite possibly, in
the future, someone will uncover evidence that will reveal what
really happened.

It was early 1937 when Charles Bell bought the parcel of land
from the farm and commissioned the construction of his new
grand estate. The children from the farm were used to crossing
the fields and playing at the opening of Joshua Creek. They were
told of the new house being built there, so they would skirt the
construction area and go play as children did, sometimes cutting

through the site to save time, as they thought it was adventurous. Who would it hurt? After all, there were many chores to be done on a farm and one had to make the most of it when given the chance to go out and play. It was late fall in 1937 when a small African-American girl named Tonya, the daughter of a servant couple at the farm, made her way to the creek. The men worked the fields as she crossed the road onto the Bell property. It was early and work had not yet begun on the construction site; the area was desolate except for one lone man, a young man who was hired to stand watch over the expensive construction materials on the site.

It was at this time that this young man, for reasons unknown, decided to attack the child crossing the property; it was her cries that brought the men running from the fields to see what had happened. Upon their arrival they found a man standing over the lifeless body of Tonya. Blind with anger, they carried both Tonya and the young man back to the farm. As they waited behind the farmhouse for the owners to come in from the back fields, Tonya's mother emerged from the kitchen. Her heart broken with despair, she collapsed next to her child, sobbing. This pushed the mob that had gathered into a frenzy, and a rope was tossed up over a low-hanging tree branch. Before the owner of the farm arrived it was already too late; the workers had extracted their justice for the child and her mother with a lynching. The farm owner arrived and was shaken by what he found; a man hung in his backyard, a dead child, a grieving mother, and an angry mob. He was first and foremost a businessman, and therefore thought the situation through. He saw there were two crimes committed: one against the poor child and one against the young man. Logically this man paid for his crime: the mob had exacted instant justice, and to call in the police would mean he would lose some of his hands and his harvest would rot in the fields. In addition, he feared that the newspapers would create a scandal that would damage the farm's reputation. Cooler heads had to prevail. They would bury the child on the farm grounds in a nice, private ceremony. As for the hanged man, he looked to the farm hands and told them, "Get rid of this body or go to jail."

They took him back to the Bell property and buried him in a shallow grave inside the newly laid foundation of the coach house. No one spoke of the incident, there were no police reports, and no news stories to research, just our recorded EVPs and the testimony of three separate and independent mediums.

APPENDIX I

TESTIMONY OF PARTICIPANTS

This book was written with extreme care in order to record every detail of all events and of the participants' experiences. I felt it would be important for the reader to hear first-hand accounts from all those who had experiences while working on this project.

There was a woman singing while we were all sitting on the stairs. She had a soft voice and I believe the music [piano] was classical. Everyone could hear it, even with the unaided ear.

— Krystal Leigh, investigator

The property was quite large and beautiful; a nice place to explore. I decided to walk just to the end of the parking lot, so as not to be alone and too far from everyone else. I was using a parabolic microphone, but only seemed to be catching the nearly deafening sounds of airplanes buzzing overhead and the occasional car on a nearby road. As I reached what was close to the very end of the parking lot, I faintly heard something, a shuffling, from inside the bushes on my right. Even with the sound-amplifying device it was nearly inaudible, so I figured I might have just imagined hearing it. To make sure it wasn't just a bird I closely approached the bushes, looking into them right through to the other side, but there was nothing there. I suddenly had a somewhat uneasy feeling and decided to go back to where the team had set up camp. I turned away from the bushes and began walking back, but before taking even five steps I felt like I was being watched. Turning back, I saw what, at first glance, I thought was another team member simply exploring the grounds like myself. I was even about to speak to them when it took a few more quick steps toward me and then stopped; I then realized it wasn't normal. It was the complete form of a man, average height and build, but in a dark, opaque, black. It seemed somewhat less dimensional than an average human and didn't possess any distinct features (eyes, nose, and mouth, outline of clothes or limb joints). The figure remained, facing me; I got the sense that it was somewhat startled that I could see it, but was also interested and curious about me. I stood watching it for a few seconds and then turned away quickly, continuing back towards the others. I looked back once more, walking backwards, and saw the figure run towards the bushes. It vanished before it hit them.

— AMANDA JOBE, JUNIOR INVESTIGATOR

During the silent period while the medium was working with the pendulum I could hear faint music, for which there was no apparent source.

— JOHN MULLAN, TECHNICAL MANAGER

During the experiment I was sitting facing the back of the house and the basement patio doors. Out of the corner of my eye I saw a shadow of a head and shoulder quickly peer in from the right side of the glass and then dart back out of sight. This happened twice.

— SHERYL POPP, CASE MANAGER

As I was listening to the clairvoyant I was sitting in a position to see down the main floor hall to the glass doors and the field beyond. It was at this time that I noticed a silhouette of a person looking toward the house, standing beside a tree. It was completely dark and had no clear edge to it — it seemed to be almost made up of black smoke. The background was bright, as everything was covered by freshly fallen snow and an exterior light was shining on it, which had made the dark figure stand out so noticeably. It lingered for a few seconds and then, in a blur of smoke, it sped away from the tree into the darkness. We immediately went out to investigate; there were no footprints in the snow.

— DARRIN LAPOINTE, FILM DIRECTOR

I was standing in the second-floor bathroom, quietly listening, when I heard what sounded like running, like a small child running, the hollow sound of a heel hitting the floor. It sounded very far away.

— LYNN PINETTE, PARTICIPANT

While prepping my camera I checked all my settings and began to run bars and tone, you know, the stuff you see late at night when a television station goes off the air. Well, I began running the bars, recording it the same way I always do, thirty seconds' worth. So at the thirty-second mark I hit the "stop" button, but it didn't stop, so I tried another "stop" button and nothing happened. I'd never had this problem before with my camera, so I thought to myself that maybe the unit froze, so I pulled the battery out and that's when things turned quite weird — my LCD viewfinder still had a picture, but there was absolutely no power running the camera. The unit stayed that way for about a minute and then reset itself. This was one of the many technical anomalies that night.

— JUSTIN MCINTOSH, FILM CREW

So many things happened that night. When we were over near the house and they were saying they saw a shadow figure and their meters were detecting something, I felt a cold chill press against my back. It was strange, the higher the meter went, the more pressure I felt against my back. When the meter dropped to zero, whatever was at my back was gone as well. Another time when we were filming near the main house I looked up at the second-floor window and saw a female there, looking out, and then she vanished. The house was locked and no one was inside, but several of the crew also saw her and as we were discussing what we had seen something grabbed me; I thought it was a vine or a cord from the equipment, but the cord was wrapped in my hand and we were standing on flagstone, nowhere near the bushes. It was a very light touch and I could definitely feel distinct fingers let go of my leg. It freaked me out.

— GRANT MACPHEE, FILM CREW

I was providing location security for the film shoot, and always professed to be a skeptic when it came to this sort of stuff. I followed the film crew up the driveway to the turning circle. I was standing there as the crew walked in front of the building and off to my right I heard a little child giggle. I immediately got goosebumps and a shiver down my spine. Needless to say, I am no longer a skeptic.

— JOHN BURNELL, PROJECT SECURITY

It was our first visit to this large estate; I left everyone and went around to the side of the house, and when I looked back toward the front of the house I was startled to see a white, luminescent form of a person standing a few metres from me on the path I had just crossed. It just stood there for a few moments, so I called out to my brother and as he approached the form started to run, but then simply vanished before my eyes.

— PAUL PALMISANO, SENIOR INVESTIGATOR

As we were sitting on the stairs I was listening to what John was saying when I heard a tapping sound very close to me, it was *tap, tap, tap*. Then it repeated again, like someone was hitting a pencil on wood. I looked around and it seemed like no one else could hear it, just me.

— MARK ROBINSON, PARTICIPANT

I was brought in as part of the film crew; my first experience that night was seeing the face of a girl who looked out of the second-floor window at us. It was brief and the house was locked up and no one was inside. As strange as that was, the other experience I had was really weird. We were walking around the mansion and you could hear everyone around you, their equipment and the leaves crackling underfoot, and then all sound stopped. I thought I had gone deaf, because we were still moving, but there wasn't a sound, not even the leaves under our feet. It was like we had entered a dead zone. All of a sudden the sounds came back — no one could explain it.

— JASON PEREZ, FILM CREW

This was a place with so much activity, the ghostly communication and sounds were all so clear during the investigation, but it was the voice of the little girl wanting her dolly that stuck in my head. At the end of the investigation when they brought her a doll and left it there, I looked up and she gave a little smile and waved good-bye; it was very moving. What I found disturbing was that around the side of the servant quarters, I could feel the ground pulling me down. I felt that someone had been murdered and buried there. The man in the servant area kept asking for help, but I sensed he wasn't a nice man and knew he would hurt me if given the chance.

— MICHELE STABLEFORD, MEDIUM

The best way to describe my experience at the house is to tell you what I went through. Hearing unexplained footsteps when I was in the kitchen, the sound of a woman's voice asking me to "Come here" when no one was there, to seeing a black image out of the corner of my eye when I was waiting for Richard and Paul to change the surveillance tape. But of all the things that I experienced, the thing I remember the most is having an overwhelming feeling of anxiety. I knew they were there and whatever they were, they knew that we were there too. Good or bad it does not matter; the fact is they knew, and it felt like we were the ones under the microscope.

— STEVEN BARWICK, INVESTIGATOR

I was standing in the hallway of this house, watching the lead investigator use his equipment to scan a room adjacent to us. I was a skeptic with very little belief in anything paranormal; however, I was very curious about the possibility of ghosts. I remained a curious skeptic until I turned my head and looked down the east hallway through a glass door. Outside were two floating orbs with bright light emanating from both. I was speechless, and no longer a skeptic. At that point it occurred to me … the orbs appeared to be just as curious as I was.

— CHRIS HARDING, ADVISER

APPENDIX II

THE SOCIAL SPIRITS

We had just finished a ten-month investigation of haunted museums and historic properties for the Museums of Mississauga when we were first introduced to the Fusion Centre. It was this house and the events of that first visit that told me this was the place to conduct an in-depth investigation. As Fusion became the focus of our attention, I didn't want this particular chapter of our investigation of Mississauga to become lost.

The reason I wanted to add this story to the book was to reveal two extremely important situations that allow us to see directly into the realm of the supernatural. The first is how a memory can be so powerful that, as it manifests, it can physically influence the living, and the second event demonstrates that spirits are social and interact with each other in a world that remains, for the most part, beyond our perception; life goes on for those who have passed over. This was demonstrated in the book where Tonya seemed to maintain a social closeness to not only those spirits in her home, but with those at Fusion as well. I found it to be a very profound discovery.

Lewis and Elizabeth Bradley built their farmhouse in 1830; the home today is a museum operated by the City of Mississauga.

The spirits there are friendly and welcoming. Relocated to the Bradley property is a house named by its first owner as the Anchorage; the structure is a fine example of Regency-style construction. It was owned by Commander John Skynner, who served under Admiral Horatio Nelson aboard his ship *Hirondelle*, battling against France and its emperor Napoleon. He settled into his home in 1839. Although Commander Skynner and the Bradleys were separated by class distinction, they all were part of the same small community known as Merigold's Point.

The reports at the Anchorage were of strange noises, lights that turned on and off without reason, doors that would close on their own, and staff were reporting dizziness and nausea.

We had just finished shooting interviews for the documentary *A Haunting* for an episode entitled "Darkness Follows" (which was based loosely on my first book *Overshadows*) with New Dominion Pictures for the Discovery Channel at the Bradley Museum when Paul and I were taking a break outside. Paul said he had seen two spirits near the rear of the old homestead. He described the man and woman he had just seen and the period clothing they were wearing. Later, we mentioned this to the curator, and she said his description fit that of the Bradleys and she would see if she could locate some photos of their original portraits for us to look at.

Although our first investigation in the Skynner house was short, it showed us that the reports from staff were valid. As we sat in the meeting room we heard heavy footfalls near the back door. The house was locked and the only people in the building were all sitting in the meeting room. As we headed up to the second floor to have a look around and take some environment measurements, we encountered strange phenomena in the room at the top of the stairs. Our first measurement of temperature was nineteen degrees Celsius, and in a matter of three minutes the room's temperature went up to thirty-one degrees. The room became not only unbearably hot, but oppressive as well. We checked to make sure the furnace had not come on, and it had not, so we could not find an answer as to why this dramatic temperature change had occurred. We retreated down to the main floor where it was cooler. It was then that we heard footfalls on the stairs. We responded and found nothing to indicate a cause. Paul and I went upstairs again and even though a relatively short period of four minutes had passed, the second floor was a comfortable nineteen degrees again.

We returned a few days later and were searching the house for anomalous electromagnetic fields. As we arrived on the second floor, everyone started to feel strange, and within a few moments we all started to experience dizziness and some mild nausea. These were the symptoms that the staff had complained about, and it seemed we now were encountering them first-hand. I just stood there and let the feeling wash over me, trying to understand what might cause these sensations. As I watched the others try and cope with the feeling I noticed something Paul did — he put his hand on the doorjamb to steady himself. I looked to each person and saw something bizarre, everyone was swaying to a rhythm, and it seemed that as each person swayed they did so in synch with each other, first right, then left. It made sense, as I realized that how we moved and felt was not unlike when one stood on a boat in rough water. Even though we were standing in the commander's house, I believed we had all been swept up in one of Skynner's memories of being out at sea. His memory was manifesting its own reality and we were experiencing those sensations.

I looked at everyone and said, "It's like we are on open water."

Everyone smiled and as we swayed on the second floor of this solid foundation house, we could feel the waves pass beneath our feet.

This was a startling revelation, for not only us, but also to the staff who worked there and felt the house move.

It was on our final visit that the second extraordinary event took place. We were all sitting in the meeting room on the main

The spirits of Lewis and Elizabeth Bradley looking in through back door at Anchorage.

floor when Paul and I kept hearing creaking noises from the floor near the back door. We had checked several times and had found nothing. I finally decided to respond by jumping out into the hall and firing my camera toward the back door. I snapped off two quick shots. Framed in the windows of the door to the foyer were two ghostly images. Later, the image was enlarged to reveal a man looking through the left glass panel and a woman looking through the right panel; they were both wearing period clothing. When Paul looked at the photo he was immediately excited, as he recognized the couple as the two spirits he had seen behind the Bradley house. When we showed the photo to the curator she said it resembled pictures she had seen of the Bradleys. She went

off to her office and came back with photos of the Bradley portraits — the similarity was startling.

We mused philosophically on what this photo meant. Could
there be a social interaction between spirits? Had the Bradleys
come over to see Skynner, or had they come over to investigate
what we were doing here? Either way, they were now visiting a
house that did not sit on this patch of land until the 1970s. This
meant that they were aware of its existence even though they
were both dead long before it had been moved here. Could that
mean they knew of and visited the commander as well?

I found it interesting that in both these cases there was a social
interaction between spirits. The children and servants at the farm
and Fusion maintained a playful co-existence. It seems to me that,
even in death, life goes on ... as if never interrupted.

APPENDIX III

FUTURE RESEARCH

It was after going over my files that I noticed a trend. In those people who have contacted me regarding ghostly phenomena, I saw that all of them, including other family members, reported an escalation in health problems, from asthma and nosebleeds to chest pain as well as a whole host of other ailments. When I followed up to see if this observation was simply a coincidence, I found that many had visited their family doctors and discovered there was nothing found to cause these medical symptoms they were describing.

I revisited my theory on how a spirit manifested by using the surrounding environment and came to some preliminary conclusions, all of which required further investigation.

MANIFESTATION

At times, in every person's life, emotions can be so intense they may become uncontrollable. I believe the trigger of a physical manifestation of a spirit is the involuntary production of a negative or positive emotion. These emotions have a strong link to, but are not limited to, the individual's memory. As the individual lives within its own memory, there will be emotionally charged events that come to the surface. Thoughts, memories, or observed occurrences can easily create a dynamic response or reaction, even on a subconscious level. How we deal with emotion in life is no different in the afterlife; feelings are formed by experience, opinions, and attitudes. The reaction to them may be extremely powerful and involuntary and may even create behaviour that is questionable and bizarre. When an entity has a strong emotion there is a shift within the electromagnetic field, causing it to polarize. When this dielectric field polarizes, it starts a chain reaction. There is an escalation to a higher wavelength from its normal operating frequency. A harmonic resonance from within this field causes a wave to form from the memory matrix. This field begins absorption of materials and energy from within the surrounding environment. The absorbed materials become coherent and oscillate in harmony. This starts to produce the exact configuration of what the entity looked like in life. As the material is pulled in from the proximity of the event, there becomes a thermal void within the area, leaving cold spots. A partial form may start to appear. Depending on its intensity, more of the form may begin to be produced. If the emotional event is terminated, the manifestation will quickly dissipate. Depending on how long the manifestation maintains its form, the observation of auditory static discharge may be heard. As well, pools of cold water may appear as condensation forms.

The amount of material collected from the surrounding environment will dictate the type of manifestation that may occur. Limited material may only allow a fog that is charged with ions. Due to the charged particles there may be light phenomena associated with this fog. Additional material will allow for more complex structures, ranging from a partial formation of the head and/or torso, right up to a solid body manifestation.

But what type of material would be used in an environment to assist with the manifestation of a spirit? Dust.

Take, for example, how certain ghosts have been named "the white or grey lady," "the brown lady," and "shadow people." The colour or hue that gives them their names may be a direct result of materials collected from their environment. Imagine a castle built of granite; one could expect to find a grey lady haunting the place, as granite dust is grey.

Household dust, or particulate matter, comes from many sources, such as dirt, pollen, moulds, bacteria, fungi, animal dander, hair, decomposing insects, lint and fibres, insulation, mites and their excrement, and human skin cells. It is estimated that forty-three million tons of dust filters down over the United States each year. Approximately 31 million tons are natural the other 12 million are man-made. Your home may even contain dust not only from all over the world, but also from outer space; space particles contribute to the increase in Earth's mass by ten thousand tons each year, and according to an article in the *New Scientist*, dust can contain pieces of DNA.

Other studies have shown that dust can contain harmful chemicals, toxins, pathogens, and known carcinogens. One study found, after analyzing the contents of a vacuum bag, thirty-five toxic industrial chemicals that were all associated with causing an assortment of health ailments, including respiratory and reproductive problems.

For example, bacteria can trigger asthma symptoms and are known to cause increased respiratory problems.

Other particles appearing in dust are chemicals found in vinyl products, components found in paint, cleaning solutions and textiles, pesticides, chemicals found in flame retardants, Teflon, Gore-Tex, fibreglass, and asbestos, to name a few.

In most cases these types of particles are not considered harmful, however, when brought together in abundance they become hazardous.

It was these particles that led me to believe coming into contact with spirits could cause us harm.

I found when the spirit is at rest it will be unperceivable, but as it becomes emotional, small changes start to occur: the field around it produces a small static field. This is what people have described as the hairs on the backs of their necks standing up. The spirit is now interacting with its environment, and as its emotion grows this field does too, and soon it is pulling in dust particles, like that of a television screen. As it grows in intensity it will leave cold spots around it because it begins to pull energy from the atmosphere, including heat. I feel at this moment that should we be in close proximity to a manifesting spirit, our health could be at risk because as the manifestation dissipates, the particles are expelled from the field and come into direct contact with us, and could spell disaster, depending on the amount and type of particles.

For example, I went out to find someone or something beyond my own files to support this theory and the first case that came to mind was a book called *The Black Hope Horror*, written by Ben Williams, Jean Williams, and John Bruce Shoemaker. The book details a haunting in which members of the Williams family come into contact with spirits and several die. I believe it to be an extreme case.

The term "ghost sickness" has been coined to explain reported illness associated by those who feel that contact with the dead has caused their conditions. The medical community has termed it "somatization disorder," in which there are numerous complaints involving pain, and problems with the respiratory, nervous, gastrointestinal, and reproductive systems where no other cause could be found to account for the symptoms.

In Aboriginal culture it is believed that the spirit causes these illnesses to take a loved one with them on their journey into life after death.

If my theory is correct, most of the symptoms can be explained by the components we are exposed to on a daily basis within our own homes. We know that most of the particles we encounter are harmless in the quantity we find around the house, however, what might be the outcome should we be bombarded by them in higher quantities, and there is an underlying part to this equation? How does the spirit's energy field affect this process?

This of course is just a working theory and it is to be understood that anyone encountering health problems should be attended to by a medical doctor. This theory is only speculative and a great deal of work lies ahead.

OTHER BOOKS BY RICHARD PALMISANO

Journeys into the Unknown
Mysterious Canadian Encounters with the Paranormal
978-1-55002-620-7
$22.99

This fascinating and bloodcurdling book takes the reader through a collection of amazing ghost stories and paranormal investigations across Ontario that have never before been reported. Other features include an examination of a complete investigation of a haunting and a guide that explains the techniques used to conduct a paranormal investigation.

Overshadows
An Investigation into a Terrifying Modern Canadian Haunting
978-1-55002-473-9
$19.99

In 1995, a young girl living with her abusive mother commits suicide. Shortly afterwards, her spirit returns to the house, only to find her mother gone and strangers moving in. She also finds the older spirits who dwell there, beginning a powerful battle for control of the house and trapping its new residents in the middle. Overshadows shares the incredible discoveries made during the course of a six-year investigation.

Available at your favourite bookseller.

 DUNDURN PRESS
www.dundurn.com

Tell us your story! What did you think of this book?
Join the conversation at www.definingcanada.ca/tell-your-story
by telling us what you think.